FROM GANGS TO GOURMET

PAUL SMITH

Copyright Paul Smith (March 2024)

All rights reserved

No part of this book may be reproduced, or stored in a retrieval system, or transmitted in any form or by any means, electronic, mechanical, photocopying, recording, or otherwise, without express written permission of the publisher

DEDICATION

Stacey, Paul, Lucas, Madison
And of course Big Angie
My Auntie Sandra and Uncle Vinny.

And a cheeky dedication to Jelly

CONTENTS

Prologue: Epiphany 1
From the Dock To The Cell 3
First Stirring Of Change 11
The Milk Wars 20
Echoes Of The Past 30
Heading For The Big League 46
Stepping Into The World Of Drugs 52
Bad Trips 56
The Isle of Skye 60
My Wrongful Conviction (2002) 195
A Year of Living Dangerously (2000) 68
gravitating towards the dark days (2001) 74
The Cranhill Days 76
Young Rogues, Young Offenders 89
It's A Set Up 94
'Watch Your Company Kid' 107
Unpredictable Life In The Schemes 113
A Significant Meeting 116
Morning After The Night Before 121
Bonnie Night (2001) 128

Karma's a Bitch	137
Aftermath (2001)	145
Bad Reputation's Stick	153
Kid-On Car Thieves	156
The Party Is Over	167
Polmont (Nov 2001)	172
Relationship With My father	188
Long Term Stretch	191
High Court	195
The Beginning Of Long Incarcerations	206
HMP Shotts	212
HMP Kilmarnock	216
Life Inside	223
Beginning Of The Change	227
The Last Hoorah	233
Short Road To Freedom	236
In Deep	240
Bang Bang, He Shot Me Down!	248
The Birth Of My First Born	254
About The Author	257

PROLOGUE: EPIPHANY

As I lay on my rock-hard bed in my Scottish prison cell, known as a 'Peter', and stared up at the top bunk, I couldn't help but think about how my life would be forever changed in just one day.

My lifelong friend, John McMillan, shouted down from the landing above me. He asked what sentence I thought I would receive, followed by another friend who asked the same question.

I replied, 'No more than eight years, surely.'

They all wished me luck.

The following morning at 6am sharp, the sound of keys jingling woke me. It was 'sentencing day'. I couldn't ignore the million thoughts racing through my mind. I was always in trouble, but I never imagined that my life would spiral out of control so quickly. Now, it was time to face the consequences.

After sipping coffee, brushing my teeth, and gelling my hair, I heard the keys getting close to my door. I met Jay, another fellow inmate who was also my best friend. Together, we would face our fate in the dock in just a few hours' time. We headed down to the holding cells to the part where the name of the court we were assigned to was listed on a whiteboard. A screw opened my door, and I thought it was time to leave, but a large man blocked my exit and wished me luck. It was Gibby's father who worked as a prison officer.

As my co-accused Gibby and Martin Graham, made their way alongside me to the dock, I watched the judge's eyes fix on each one of us in turn. He sat there with the power to lock us up for a hundred years if he so felt like it. Sentencing was over quickly, but it marked the end of my old life.

From that point forward, I would be known as prisoner 66680.

This experience made me reflect on who I was, where I came from, and the choices that led me to this point.

.oOo.

This book contains many stories of violence, humour, love, drink, drugs, police doing their job, and others who live to make your day miserable. Unfortunately, some stories will also involve death, including the painful experience of suicide, which I always wonder if I could have prevented. And most importantly, the wrongful conviction I received for a robbery I had nothing to do with.

FROM THE DOCK TO THE CELL

For me life turned into colour with the sound of the 90's rave scene. Teenagers swaggered from street to street with rave music or Happy Hardcore as it was more commonly known blaring out of their ghetto blasters with the heat of summer in full swing. Men drank cans of lager stamped with half-naked ladies, and almost all the youths had posters plastered over their bedroom walls with the big letter Z on them (the Z standing for the Resurrection).

The rave scene might have been in full swing but for us it was just out of reach. We were still a bunch of piss-ant kids without a hair on our pencils. There was no doorman this side of the Mississippi that would have ever let us anywhere near the Rez. So, unfortunately, listening to it on the ghetto blaster was probably the best we could have hoped for. To us we were the second coming and desperate to get involved regardless of age, but for now anyway we could merely sit on the side lines and watch.

I remember back then one of our favourite things to do would be to go around to the McKnight brothers' house, James, and John. John being the older of them and already big into rave scene along with all the crazy clothing everyone wore, all bright colours and baggy bottoms with bucket hats and sunglasses - no matter the time of year. Ecstasy was flying around at that time, those little white wonder pills that would make your jaw shoot out like an office drawer and let's not forget they would make your eyes bounce about your head;

people looking at you would think you were watching a Wimbledon final at super speed, not mention the fact they turn very black, almost no whites left just two big pupils. Then the music hit you and suddenly you turned into old snake hips moving uncontrollably to the beat. Yes, it's safe to say the 90s was a hell of a decade for anyone involved.

Unfortunately, for us, all we could do was watch. In my little mind there couldn't have been the whole ravers' movement without me and my little crew. God we were daft back then. If I am being completely honest, I may have talked a good game, but I was always very cautious or even outright scared to try things like alcohol and especially illegal drugs.

This was around the years of 1995/1996 so I would have been between the ages of 12 or 13 but in my head, I felt a lot older plus, you know how peer pressure can be, it's a very intimidating thing to any young boy especially one who was always running around with older lads trying hard to fit in and be considered an equal.

Back then we were all thick as thieves and loyal as hell to one another. There was me, James McKnight, Mick McCrann, John Frazer, and a dozen or so more. We were close, as kids tend to be, running mad without a care in the world.

Then everyone started to drink and try new things like small amounts of hash. I hated it. In my opinion it is the worst drug ever to infiltrate society. That is just my take on it, not that it should be carved in stone on Temple Mount.

Other stuff came later, but at this time all we were concerned with was girls and having fun with the boys. I guess in our way we all thought we had the world by the balls. Youth is a hell of a thing!

Yet to even imagine having the world at your feet, no matter how small your little circle is, you still need money. We were anything but afraid to go out and make as much of it as we could. That was when t I realised that I was a pretty good thief. As with some kids, shoplifting was always a good place to start. So, on top of petty vandalism, I added shoplifting to my now expanding criminal resume. And believe me there wasn't a shop we didn't hit, from Dixons to RS McColl's and every shop in between.

In shops like Dixon's the only real obstacle was the old glass case with the slide open door, nothing hard there, apart from getting to it in the first place. You see it always had a member of staff standing guard, usually some new start doing his YTS (Youth Training Scheme) but we knew how to divide and conquor. We'd usually go into the shop in sets of five or six with the one who was nominated to make the snatch going in on their own.

The gang would walk around looking as if they were into stealing stuff. And right on cue this pizza-faced kid that took his job way too seriously, would walk over like Rambo thinking "Yeah! I'm going to single handedly toss all these wee thieving shits out on their asses." All the while, the one who all eyes should be on, was walking around without a care in the world. So, while Mr Big Shot and his £3.20 an hour wage went to confront the young team, our boy on point was loading up with Walkmans, Disc Mans, cameras, and basically anything else he could stick in his bag and then he just walked right out the door.

Even though are type of products were all security tagged up the wazoo and the alarms would usually go off, the staff were always more interested in the NEDs standing at the doors making a scene. So they wouldn't give two shits about anything else. Then off our designated theif went, straight out the door with their bag of loot.

The next job was to go and sell the lot. All these things at the time were very hot indeed to us. Discmans were like the iPhones of today. Everyone had, or wanted, one. Those things were always a very easy sell. And no sooner had we offloaded them - usually in the Carbrain area of our beloved hometown - we would hop a bus into Glasgow to hit HMV, a very popular music store. We would run through the place like a swarm of locusts grabbing as many Titanic videos as we could. That video was the top of every girl's wish list that year, thank you, Mr Leonardo DiCaprio. Then we'd get the hell out of dodge.

Videos tapes back then where as big as encyclopedias, so sticking seven, maybe even eight, up and around your jumper at any one time was no easy task. You ended up walking out the door like a fucking Transformer. All the security guards pissing themselves laughing at each other saying, "There goes Optimus Prime again." But for the most part we usually did it without incident.

From there we elevated to filling trolleys full of booze topped off with sweets and crisps just to camouflage the real prizes underneath and walk straight out the doors of local supermarkets. Basically, what we would do is go into stores like Asda and Tesco always with an older woman who we will just call "the blonde one." So me and another boy called John F would go in with the blonde one just like any other happy shoppers, right into the spirit aisle. We would fill the bottom half of the trolley with all things over 40% proof and sometimes even bottles of Moet Champagne if it was the weekend, and we wanted to look like kings while acting like idiots. Clowns or not, everyone wanted to be around you when you're sitting in the local swing park swigging down bottles of champagne.

I guarantee you one thing, getting a girlfriend, even if only for the night, was a hell of a lot easier with a bottle of Moet in your hand than just a cheeky grin. Remember we were like fourteen at this point, so I wouldn't use it as a foolproof plan in your average daily search for love. As for the rest of the loot, we had a house in the Carbrain area that would take the lot every time without fail. This old woman had people on standby, ready to buy anything we could grab, right there and then. She had a queue of people out the door and around the block, all waiting to take all the booze and joints of meat, along with anything else we could get our hands on. Well, who doesn't love a bargain? Without question, the money was always there no matter how much we brought down to her, trolley load after trolley load, filled with booze, meat, and electrical devices - almost daily.

Back then things like video players, ghetto blasters, even drills and other DIY tools were all in their original packaging. Granted, they came with security tags, but you could just pull them off without any resistance. Back then we were getting around £250 per trip but that was to go four ways: myself, John F, the blonde one, and Wee Eck.

Wee Eck was a funny-sounding, bubbly guy who sometimes drove us around to different stores throughout the Strathclyde area. When some shops in Cumbernauld started to notice our faces, and you'd get that gut feeling you were being watched, we just knew to walk out the door and move on to another shop; that's where Wee Eck would come in. He just drove us elsewhere without question.

Our little Cumbernauld crime wave went on for about a year or so without getting pinched and in its own way was somewhat successful. Only then we started getting a taste for the money and better things. You know, having money, no matter how little or a lot, always makes you feel better, act better, and basically be a better person. Not having it and bang, you're back on the bread line pissing about waiting for the weekend with the hope of better things to come. This was around the summertime of 1996 when the shit finally hit the fan. Well, it did for me and John anyway.

We had decided to hit Tesco, not the smartest thing to do as we had been hitting this same store now consistently for weeks, and before we even got there my radar was up. I just didn't like the thought of it one bit but greed had gotten the best of the other three. Even though Wee Eck always stayed safely in the car and the blonde one walked out the doors well before any crime was ever committed leaving only me and John to do the bit - my vote to go elsewhere was all but ignored and off we went. As usual, the blonde one fueled up the trolley then left the shop, with us two walking out five minutes or so behind her, no problem we thought, just another trolley load out and away.

Only this time, as soon as we passed the fresh food, the security grabbed me first. I managed to pull free and took off running through the car park. John took off like a fucking shot and was all but home free. As for me, well, the security guard was hot on my heels, let's just say he definitely had his Weetabix that morning. He was like a fucking track star and was all over me like a rash before I could say "tickety-boo."

I was taken into the security room in the back of Tesco kicking and screaming while they were calling the police. They tried to get my wee sidekick's name from me, only for one of them to butt in and say, "You're not going to believe this, the other one just walked back in the store and gave himself up."

Why? To this day I have no answer — and never have one now as John has been dead a few years. John for some reason handed himself back in and we were both arrested and taken home and charged. Then the police just left us at home.

I remember thinking "Fuck me, are they just leaving? Really, is that all that happens if you get caught?" I mean we were grabbed with over four hundred pounds of stolen shit in that trolley and they're just taking us home. Honestly, I don't know what I thought the consequences would be but nothing ever did happen. Getting arrested for the first time is a bit like losing your virginity, a big fucking let down. You build this image up in your mind then when it happens you think, "Was that it?" Of course, it depends on what you're pinched for. I can't imagine being arrested for something like murder would be a cake walk but, thankfully, I've only come close to that before and never went too far.

My mother, on the other hand, that was a different story. She was demanding that I tell her who this woman was, the one we called "the blonde one", what was her name, where did she stay? Stuff like that. (Aye right, so I fuckin will.) Like they say in Goodfellas, never rat on your friends and always keep your mouth shut. To this day I don't believe she knows who the blonde one was, and she never will, not by my admission anyway.

With 1996 turning into 1997, a bunch of boys who thought we would stay together for life, started to break apart one by one. We went our separate ways until the once mighty group was all but a shell of itself. I started running around in Carbrain full time. I had kind of dipped my toes in and out, but it was time to just dive in. James and Mick stayed together down the Seafar, running around with what was left of them. John came back down to Carbrain, but not within the same group as me. As for the rest, god only knows. The point is we all lost touch, though I will always consider them my friends

Our little group in Carbrain consisted of myself, KitKat, the McKinnon brothers Andy and Scott, and their tag-along younger brother Russell. Not to mention Starky, Humbug's sister Gillian, a few of her friends, and, finally, Chris Barkley (whose mother, as coincidence would have it, is still my lawyer's secretary, called Margaret). That was our little gang of guys, though me and Andy were always closer than most because he was schooling me in committing crimes, leading me into a lot more serious stuff than just shoplifting.

FIRST STIRRING OF CHANGE

1997, it was a great year. We had Oasis topping the charts almost daily with more hits than a mafia Don's arrest sheet. Mulder and Scully were still out there trying to find the truth. And even our beloved Blackpool was still the go-to destination for stay-at-home Brits. Most importantly, in my opinion, '97 was the year I got my first taste of High School.

Our Lady's High School Cumbernauld was the nearest Roman Catholic school to us, not that the RC element had much to do with it. There were atheists out there who were more religious than the Smith family. However, in those days, if you were Catholic, you went to a Catholic primary, then the same for your secondary - and that was that. So, Our Lady's was the place for me. It was an old building constructed back in 1968, and not much had changed since its grand opening. Maybe a new chair here or a splash of paint there, but that was about it. The council was not big in prioritising things like schools, playparks, or any other quality of life essentials in our area. That said, the night before I couldn't sleep with the excitement.

Then the day finally came, Christ almighty, I was a high school student, diving headfirst into my teenage years full of innocence and anticipation without a care in the world and hoping that all the bullshit from my time at primary was at an end. Thinking for some reason that my dyslexia troubles were over. Why I thought that, I don't know. Wishful thinking perhaps, but alas, it was not to be.

Day one was full of excitement & wonder. Everyone went out of their way to go above and beyond, and they were all extra friendly to you. All the staff from teachers to dinner ladies, even janitors, not to mention all the fifth and sixth-year students, everyone in the building going that extra wee mile to make all new first year pupils feel warm and welcomed.

It's funny to think, but in just three short years of this date, I would go from that skinny, pizza-faced angel to being spattered over the national papers with headlines like 'Cumbernauld Thugs go on summer rampage.' It always amazes me just how fast your life can take a sharp left into dangerous waters without warning. Thankfully, that was three years away and there was enough to fill three lifetimes in between.

Meanwhile, back in high school, I was finding my feet like most kids. We were quickly getting to know one another despite being from different schools and starting to learn about a range of new subjects. Meanwhile, I was praying that I wouldn't be asked any questions, especially in front of the class, you see dyslexia wasn't my only challenge, I also had crippling shyness and very low confidence. All three would go on to follow me throughout my life, with them still haunting me to this day.

Even sitting here today writing this book wasn't something that happened over night, the decision to even make a start on it took years and probably wouldn't have come to pass if it wasn't for my friend and editor Lea Taylor who is always pushing me in new directions to face my self-doubt and confidence issues. So, for someone like me getting asked to stand and read something out loud to the whole class was stuff of nightmares. Back in those days schools didn't even test for things like dyslexia until the high school age, so by then most of the damage had already been done.

An anti-authority attitude can very easily develop and become ingrained in you. That's what happened with me and countless others because we sat there feeling stupid. So, we tended to find other ways of shining in class; the class clown was one route, another often was aggression and yet another was simply to just not show up. These things were not just down to the student deciding he/she was just giving up on school.

The staffing body was, if you ask me, always far too quick to label and move them on as uninterested or disruptive. Very rarely do we see classes taking the time to dig deeper into root causes. A common misconception is that having learning difficulties - such as dyslexia, dyscalculia, or what we know now as ADHD - means the person is stupid. This cannot be further from the truth. The fact is they just have better skills elsewhere. As for me, I found my place in the kitchen as a chef and now as a writer. Because I sucked balls at Math's and English the schools where happy to let me fuck about in class or even better (in their books) when I couldn't be arsed coming in at all.

Far too many kids, year after year, are slipping through the cracks because all the education board wants to hear about are the school's top scoring pupils. To this day. Nothing changed there, and it pisses me off.

As hard as school was there some subjects I thrived in. History, for one, was a class I would attend on a regular basis. There was something good I got from learning about the past, it caught my attention, don't ask me why it just did. As George Santayana said, Those who cannot remember history are doomed to repeat it" and, of course, Home Economics was a class I never missed. The rest I am sad to say, fell by the wayside.

Still, I had my happy moments and plenty of them. Plus, my two friends who I ran with outside of school, James, and Michael McCrann, attended the same place as me. And even though they were a few years ahead of me we would still kick about on our lunch under the Janitor's open-air garage smoking cigarettes, both the legal and the illegal kind. Going back to classes stoned and, even though I was always forcing every drag of that stinky shit down my throat to fit in or to look just a little bit older in some girl's eyes, I never truly enjoyed it. In fact, it's safe to say I down right hated the stuff.

Then, something weird starting happening, probably because we were doing it in the middle of the school day with the thrill of getting caught, I came to find myself chasing it more and more. That became the real buzz for me. I started to feel like James Dean a real rebel. Apart from that I got no enjoyment from it whatsoever.

That 'do anything for a kick,' thrill seeking attitude was my real addiction and would follow me through life. Though, my idea of going out for kicks these days is deciding if we are doing our shopping on a Friday night or Saturday morning- 'good times,' it's still in me.

As for James and Mick, they were Cumbernauld's answer to Cheech and Chong. They smoked that shit morning, noon, and night, and I felt obligated to try and keep up with them. Until it all came crashing down one rainy Monday afternoon. I had been taking buckets at lunchtime in the wooded area behind the school. When lunch ended, around ten or so of us tripped back to our classes.

Even before I hit the school grounds, I was starting to go whiter and whiter. Yes, ladies and gentlemen, I was hitting a whitey – the sick just waiting for the perfect moment to meet the world.

To make matters worse, my class was on the top floor and the bathroom on the bottom. Anyway, it wouldn't have made a difference. I was sick all over the teacher's table, the floor, and thankfully just a little on a lassie's shoes.

After the teacher came over, with that *Jesus Christ young man, are you okay* look on his face. He took one look at my red, bloodshot, fiery eyes and ordered me out of the class. By then, I was feeling much better. As he shouted in my face, 'Are you on drugs?' I couldn't do anything but slide down the wall laughing at him. That was it – down to the headmaster's office and out the door on a 14-day suspension. My first-ever suspension, and they hit me with fourteen to be days stuck with my mother Angie – talk about hell on wheels! Fourteen days of constant ear bending. The rest of '97 was nowhere near as bad after that.

By the summer of that year, I was already drinking every weekend with random females in my sights – as I suppose any young whipper snapper does at that age. I could talk big but at the same time, knowing absolutely nothing about what makes a girl tick. Not that it wasn't fun finding out. Around this time, I started going with my first semi-serious girlfriend, Leanne Mack. Not that it lasted very long – about two weeks, I think, with nine days of that spent arguing, and the rest I was pissed.

Five minutes after we split, my mate Ginger was right in there, thinking he was 'books in,' not knowing our wee mate William P was already in there. Now, don't think for a minute that I am calling her any sort of tart because she was the furthest thing from that – believe me. A few of us tried, but she was determined to keep her chastity.

As summer turned to autumn, I started to turn to more crime, drink, and drugs – still soft drugs initially but fast racing towards ecstasy, or sweeties, as they are known.

The '90s was our summer of love – where the hippies of the '60s had hash, LSD, and free love, we had loud music, ectos, and car thieves. Cumbernauld, at this time, had a bad problem with people's car's being stolen. It all came down to one person. A boy I would become friends with only a few years later and who showed me the basics in the art of stealing cars. This wasn't some 'Gone in sixty seconds' stuff, nothing at all like that. Just a bunch of teenagers running around in cars that didn't belong to them. We were, at that stage, still on the outside looking in, thinking, and dreaming of being part of the coolest looking kids on the streets.

.oOo.

One time that always stands out was around the end of the summer that year. A boy called Foye and three or so more of what was known back then as the YCCT (Young Carbrain Car Thieves) came racing down Stonylee Road with Cumbernauld's police chasing them. As he took the sharp right at the bottom of the street, heading fast into what seemed like a dead-end, trailing police cars with flashing lights who must have thought to themselves, *here it comes, get ready for the arrest.* you could almost imagine them salivating with the excitement of finally getting him banged to rights.

What came next was totally unexpected. Foye mounted the curb onto the path, past the wee shop, and did something that made him a five-minute legend. There was a double set of stairs just outside Jazz's shop; he lined the car up perfectly and drove down them, down the long path on to the road at the bottom. Witness ten or so of us impressionable young ones, with the police left standing, looking completely stunned.

Nowadays, like most fathers, I would be raging at the thought that some wee cock was so reckless driving like that where kids usually played, but at the time, he was 'the man'. I never found out if the police caught up with him for the stunt he pulled or not. It would still be another eighteen months or so before we started running with him.

Just after my fourteenth birthday, I took my ecto, and half a Mitsubishi. It all came about from my friend at the time, Scott McKinnon, the middle brother of Andy, Russell, and Gordon. The weekend before, Scott had disappeared with a girl, Kirsty M, who was already into them in a big way. He took one with her; the older boys and girls were there. The way he described it to me on the Monday, OMG, I think if he kept talking about these magical little white wonder drugs, I would have gotten a hard-on right there and then. So, this was it, standing underneath B Block in Cumbernauld High School. I decided this weekend coming, I'm dropping my first E. The rest of the week was full of excitement and wonder mixed in with fear and doubt; all the time thinking of the tragic death of Leah Betts, the Essex teenager who died in November 1995. Her photo had been splattered all over the tabloids for weeks with headlines like 'This is the danger of drugs.'

Finally, Friday night came, armed with my half an E and a bottle of Buckfast, I was standing in what is known locally as The Gilly, a long stretch of woodland path where thirty or so of us always congregated at the weekends back in the days of underage drinking and general naughtiness of all kinds. God, they were the days!

Around 7 o'clock or so, there I was, standing, looking down at this little half of white pill, thinking, 'What if this happens?

What if that happens?' In the end, I just said, 'Fuck it, why not?' and dropped it down to Chinatown. Five minutes passed, and I'm thinking, 'This is shite. Scott's just a fucking liar.'

I was expecting it to hit me at the same speed as other drugs, like with hash, you can feel its effects almost instantly. Not knowing tablets of any kind, I didn't know that they usually took around 20 minutes to hit you.

Then, out of nowhere, I started to feel a tingling in my toes, working its way slowly up my body.

Someone came up with the idea to go down to the Oasis chip shop. Not the best place to go. On MDMA, the smell of greasy chips doesn't go very well, believe me. On the plus side, the chippy had a toilet in it. By the time the ectos hit my stomach, they put me in a bad position where I had to find a toilet or call the night off early due to unforeseen stinky eruptions. Thankfully I found a toilet in time, and the crisis was averted. However, as I was washing my hands, bang, the full bet of E hit me like a freight train, my eyes were like ping-pong balls bouncing back and forth inside my ears. Christ be to God, I was completely fucking wasted, struggling to find the bathroom door handle.

'Right Candy Ball, get a fucking grip. You're stuck in a chip shop bathroom due to the fact that you're smashed.' I muttered to myself, realizing that I couldn't see the handle. Finally, after what felt like an hour, I managed to open the door only to find six of my friends outside, pissing themselves at the thought of me trying to get out of an unlocked bathroom.

You know, I'm not much of a religious guy, but that night, I got as close to God as chemically possible. It was incredible, and all I could think was that I never wanted this feeling to end. Deep down, I knew that one day, like anything else, it would have to end, and I would have to face the bright, blinding light of dawn. In that moment, I felt free from all the bullshit of life, and I loved everyone. It was a very pleasant side effect from these little white wonders.

Before I knew it, Saturday morning arrived, and I was about to experience what my first comedown was all about. Fuck me, it was nasty; it's very true what they say, what goes up must come down. By then, I was already hooked.

Week after week, I sat in class, waiting for the Friday bell to ring and another weekend of madness. Unfortunately, the weekends started to roll into weekdays, and the school started falling by the wayside.

As we approached 1998, the school was all but out of the picture.

THE MILK WARS

In the eyes of my stepfather, turning thirteen meant I was a man. Well, within the world of work anyway. Forget the small fact that I was yet to sprout a single hair on my chin my armpits or dare I say even the old ball sack. To him, that would have made little difference, in his opinion I was old enough to go out and bring home the bacon.

Alex was far from an evil man. His interest in pushing me into the world of manual labour had nothing to do with doling out punishment but more about teaching me the importance of having money in my pocket. That was his upbringing, and he added it to his own parenting playbook.

He grew up in a household where going out and putting in a day's graft was not only asked but expected, and if this was the way he brought me and my brother up, so be it.

Was Alex a tough man? Yes, now and then, I mean whose old man isn't? If he saw you doing your bit, getting up every morning, going out to work, come payday, he wouldn't even take digs money, but if you started missing days, he would leave you penniless. You'd be surprised just how quickly it made you sharpen up your shit, believe me.

In his view, if you wanted the finer things in life, you got your arse up in the mornings go out and put in a graft, that simple. These are lessons I've carried with me and have adapted into my own parent planner and tried it on my own children. Unfortunately, for the most part, it falls on deaf ears.

My only hope is that they will go into the world of work with the same attitude Alex passed on to me all those years ago.

My day would start 3:44am every morning sharp, Monday to Saturday. Going from the milk van straight into School. Every day except for Saturdays, I was late. Every day I was tired and sore. Thinking back to the good old days, freezing cold, bouncing around the back of that van, they were without doubt some of the best times of my life.

I had money in my skyrocket. A very small amount granted, but still an honest day's work.

The pay packet was great but for me the more important thing was the respect. I felt respect. Respect I wouldn't find again, not until I came back home and straightened my shit out from constantly living life on the wild side.

My only wish from the mad old days was that I had put all that wasted energy into a professional kitchen, into becoming the best chef I ever could be.

You see that right there that was my real dream. Not that shit that was not a dream that was a fucking nightmare.

Who knows, I could have shot for the stars like all my heroes, people like Chef Marco Pierre White or my all-time hero Sir Albert Roux and his son Michel Roux Jr, Andrew Fairlie and so many others of the of the 20th century.

Unfortunately, I spent my youth fucking about with friends drinking wine misusing Class A's, doing almost anything to pass the time and kill the boredom. Whereas I could have and should have spent the time in a kitchen, preferably one in the Royal Navy. Even as a young whipper snapper I dreamed of one day making it into the Royal Navy as a chef but that was me a born fuck up, pissed all my dreams away and for what? Drink, drugs and the occasional dick licking from any and every available female on a Friday night.

Going back to my old milk round, there was something very appealing about standing there in the bare arse cold, the streets still dark with just a touch of the morning sun rising in the black sky as I waited to get picked up. Plus, all the boys in the van were my mates. The McKinnon brothers Andy and Scott, Chris Barclay, and Starky. All of us just having a giggle getting the job done. It was fabulous.

Then came the milk wars.

Glasgow's TC Campbell and Joe Steel had the ice cream wars, which sadly led to not only the murder of six members of the Doyle family and Scotland's biggest miscarriage of justice but also a deep distrust of Strathclyde Police which is still felt to this day.

Our little war was nothing like that, nothing at all.

So please don't strap yourself in thinking fuck me, I've never seen anything about this on YouTube before, or you will be sadly let down. Anyway, there were approximately four milk vans out there every morning covering the whole of Cumbernauld. That equates to around twenty youths coming from four or five different schemes that didn't like each other.

Like most conflicts, it started off small. You did your drop, got back in the van. Then here comes another van from another company full of boys who knew that the milk brand came from the Carbrain Van. Needless to say, the milk bottles were anything but safe with the only real victim being the poor customer and his dry bowl of Cornflakes. Still, this period of calm couldn't last forever, and gradually, it became more destructive and illegal - peoples' properties were now getting targeted, their cars damaged; we even caught some evil wee bastard pissing in a bottle of apple juice.

Then, one morning, as we jumped off the milk van, we came to a house with red paint poured all over the driveway and CYF written across the walls in the biggest letters you have ever seen. I was stunned. This was some poor person's home, totally wrecked, and for what? This was too much. Whoever did this had gone a step too far. The fact that we were in the middle of bandit country (Greenfaulds) gave us our biggest clue who did it.

Years later I asked Jay about it he confirmed that they all walked up around 2am, paint can in hand, swaggering like John Travolta. The house was picked at random, one they knew we delivered milk to and just went at it.

As he told me he roared with laughter. He laughed even more as he told me that they were literally hiding in a bush watching us when we discovered what they had done, and the shock was evident on our faces. This was just the first step in what would become a stupid tit-for-tat bullshit little grievance.

It never ended that way though, that came later in the form of a brick to Christopher's head and a 9am trip to the hospital.

As for that morning, standing there trying not to get any red paint on our trainers, we spoke about what we should do. Do we just drop the milk and move on? Do we chap the door to give them the worst wake-up call ever? Or do we find out who did this and target one of their homes? Thankfully that idea never made it off the table. As we all stood there, I guess our driver must have thought, those dirty skiving bastards were hiding somewhere and so decided to drive around to our last drop-off point.

'What the FUCK,' he bellowed from the van. His face was so red it almost melted the top off the van's roof. Before we knew it, he was out of the van and right over to us, demanding to know who did that.

Immediately we all went straight on the defence. 'None of us.' He just looked us up and down.

'Of course, none of us done it you fucking idiot. The question is, who did it? And what gang is the CYF?' We all stood there trying not to look him in the eye. 'Fuck it.' He marched up the driveway and began banging on the door. It was around six or seven am, the sun was coming up, giving the street that fresh morning look.

The door opens, a man in his maybe 40s still half asleep with that what-the-hell-do-you-want look on his face. God almighty, we all thought our driver looked mad - this guy's face was a deeper red than the paint used to vandalise his home. He was like a man possessed. I honestly thought this big bastard was going to start blaming us. Thankfully, all that happened was he turned around and stormed in, slamming his door and shouting to stay there until the police got there. We were all left standing, looking at each other.

I mean, we felt sorry for this poor guy, but ratting people out to Cumbernauld Polis, sorry mate, you have the wrong guys here. Even if we knew anything ratting on people was not in our DNA.

It never came to that. Our van driver had a run to get through, and if this guy thought that something as small as his home getting turned into the kennel for Clifford, the big red dog, he was sadly mistaken.

'Right boys, back in the van.'

I couldn't believe my ears, there we were looking at this poor guy's house totally wrecked, and our driver couldn't give two fucks.

His main objective that morning wasn't helping to get this man justice or even flying around his run in record time. No, it was the month of March, and he was desperate to get to the bookies as early as possible. If you wanted to place a bet on the Cheltenham Gold Cup, held every March, you needed to get in quick. After all, this all happened before mobile phones, let alone online betting.

If I was lucky enough to get that seat, it's because I sat in the front seat and listened to him shouting at the radio, cheering on some donkey, that I got the kick I have today for the old GGs. He and my old man Alex are both responsible for that.

When the driver told us the real reason why we were fucking off before any polis came, we rolled about the van in hysterics. I just couldn't get over the fact he was more interested in the ponies than this guy's home. It was madness, pure madness.

What happened next was anything but funny. Friday night was always the night we did the milk money collections, and unlike doing our morning deliveries, we all did it on foot. Scott and I got stuck with Westerwood, an up-your-own-arse private housing estate full of two-bob-snobs. I say two-bob-snobs because most of these arseholes are not living the dream. Real two cars in the driveway, no milk in the fridge, sort of people. No pun intended. So, getting a tip out of these wankers was slim at best.

Right off the bat, we were pissed off that we got stuck with these arseholes.

Not to mention, it was almost all uphill. What could we do? Andy and Chris Barclay were both older and had more experience, and Andy had the driver's ear.

So off we all went into our different schemes. And, just as we anticipated, door after door with next to zero tips. Around four fucking hours we spent up there and we were lucky to have enough tips to buy a bottle between us, forget the fags and drugs. Granted, we got our wages from the milk paid to us the day before, but money jumps out of your pocket at that age.

As we did our rounds, Scott smoked joint after joint of that horrible stinking hash, which made our journey all the more irritating. Finally, our nightmare was over, and we headed for the familiar streets of home.

When we got to Bells, the local off-sales, Andy and Barclay, were standing and looking weirdly spooked. The story was they had been robbed of all the milk takings. Yeah right! Scott and I thought we smelled a rat there while thinking about what a good idea it was. More importantly, why the fuck didn't we think of that? We spent the full night drilling them until, finally, they buckled and broke down with laughter. And then the bragging began.

'Do yous honestly think anyone is going to rob us? Please!'

'But what about Alan our van driver? What are you going to say to him?'

'No problem,' said Andy, 'we will just say a pair of smackheads gabbed us at needlepoint and took all of our shit.'

I wondered, could it be that easy? Well, if one boy knows Andy does. We were both thieving little shites but it was Andy who showed me the ropes. If I trusted anyone when it came to illegal shit it was him. Lo and behold, come Monday morning, he played that driver like a goddam fiddle, and that was all the excuse me and I needed.

A quick blackeye and we could keep all the week's milk-taking, close to five hundred doubloons. In those days it was a lot of money, not like today. Mind you, today, a monkey barely covers the cost of a week's shopping, but back then, two hundred and fifty each was more than a week's wages for some adults.

The only thing left to discuss was who would be lucky enough to receive the five-hundred-pound punch. Scott's answer was simple: I'm older, so I'll be flinging the knockout blow. Seniority does suck balls sometimes.

So, the plan was set for the following Friday. I was to stand there like a chump while fucking Sugar Ray Mckinnon pulled out all the stops and beat on my ass like a Bongo drum. I have to say it, sitting there waiting a full seven days for an ass whooping, real or not, was the longest week of my life. Taking a punch in life is no big deal. Why? Simple, unless you're a professional boxer; for the most part, people don't know it's coming, so the fear factor isn't there. This was different, though; not only did I know it was coming, I had a full week to think about it.

Finally, Friday came. We had done our rounds and collected the week's pay. I only had one request: ' Make it quick,' and 'I don't want to know when it's coming. Just turn and smack me one. Hit me straight on the nose.' That should, in theory, turn my eyes a nice shade of purple and black. The plan was simple; Scott's aim, not so much.

The dumb shit couldn't hit fish in a barrel. Three hits before finally he cracked me on the sweet spot. My nose opened like the Hoover Dam bursting its banks. We split the money. Thus far everything was going to plan. Just one thing remained: inform the driver.

It didn't occur to us that it looked suspect that within two weeks four of the driver's boys had been robbed. In hindsight, we should have at least waited a few weeks, let the dust settle before pulling the same shit the other two had just pulled, but greed and youth can be a dangerous combination.

Just as soon as we told Alan a bunch of the young team from the Village area attacked and robbed us. He just shook his head and mumbled under his voice greedy wee bastard couldn't even be trusted to do this. We knew we fucked up. We knew chances were that we would no doubt get the bullet by the end of the week.

He did all he could, I suppose. He called the police, and they came down to take a statement right at the side of the road. So, there's Scott and me standing there trying to think of some lie to tell them. A dummy story was given.

They knew we were full of shit but the blackeye at least gave it some credibility. Who were we kidding, everyone there knew we were full of shit. Fuck, even the fags we were smoking in the van that morning were paid for from the stolen money.

Just as we predicted, come Friday we both got the bump. Angry and stupidly, Scott and I decided to go out and do the same again, only this time, we hit basically every house in the Cumbernauld area for almost two grand in pure profit, and boom, we disappeared like a fart in the wind.

On reflection, I felt pretty shitty about that. At the time we loved it, thinking we were Cumbernauld's answer to Ronnie Biggs. Then came the remorse and fear. Remorse because even though the guy gave us the sack, he also gave us a start, and for the most part, he was a decent guy. And the fear part was because we knew the polis would definitely be involved this time, taking a lot more interest in these so-called robberies.

Following this, Andy Starky and Barclay got sacked. The company said none of us were to be trusted - the driver told them that a few heavies were the real guys behind the company and that if we were smart, we would get the money back to him before anyone started coming to our homes.

In a nutshell, he was trying to put the fear of God into us.

Even if we still had the cash, which I don't believe we did, giving it back to him was no guarantee he would walk in and pay it back. Chances were it would have gone on some three-legged disaster of a so-called horse, and we would still be left out in the cold, his word against ours. So, no matter what was going to happen the money was gone.

Nothing ever did happen. Well, the five of us fell out for a short while, but that was it and even then, we were still out on the rob at night. It was just during the day we kind of walked past each other as if we hardly knew one another. Within a few weeks, we were all back to being best mates.

Andy had another younger brother, Russell. Right back from the start I hated him. He was just a wee prick with a cunt of an attitude, and no matter what we did, we just could not get on with each other.

In the beginning, it made little difference. I was kicking about with Scott and Andy, with him trying to tag along. He was a bit of a pest, but not the worst guy to be around then. Little by little, we grew to hate one another.

ECHOES OF THE PAST

Looking back, a lot of shit happened in '97, from deaths and drugs to school screw-ups, booze and of course, battlefields. I guess it's safe to say that it left a lasting effect on me. Finally, Hogmanay came, and as the bells rang out, it was out of the old and in with the new. 1998 started with a bang for me, and, believe me, when I say this, I meant every goddamn word of that.

It all started just before 1am on New Year's Day. Someone must have mistaken my head for a baseball – okay, an easy mistake, I guess – and he goes and cracks me just behind the left ear. Whack! Fuck me, what happened there? My head rang like a bell.

Now, I can't tell you a lot about what happened that night or why Babe Ruth was running around Cumbernauld at one in the fuckin morning, handing out ass-whippings to unsuspecting teenagers, not that I don't want to tell anyone this story, more that I don't remember much about it. Nothing like a half bottle of vodka, two cans of beer and a mild concussion to mess with the old memory bank, but I will give it a crack as best I can. (No pun intended).

So, not long after the ring-a-ding-ding bells brought in 1998, we, like most people back then, took to the streets to spread cheer, drink, and be merry. This was back when people celebrated New Year, unlike today, when you would be lucky to find pubs open past 11.30pm, Hogmanay or not. So, here we are, me, the McKinnon brothers, Scott, and his younger brother Russell, who I always hated, even as kids I never had much time for the boy. Gary Bryson, Kev Williamson, Kirsty Monaghan, Darren Mills, and a dozen or so more, all out having fun, making noise, and just having a good time.

Out of nowhere, a fight broke out. Now who started it or who was even involved, I honestly can't say. All I remember is that prick giving me a crack round the side of the head with a very large bat, then thankfully, someone grabbed me out of the danger zone (who I can't remember) before this prick lined up to take a second swing. Just at that, we took off on foot by the Glenhove shop tunnel, heading back down towards Millcroft Road, thinking to myself, *what the fuck was that all about?*

I remember being taken into someone's house, again, whose house, or even what street it was in Millcroft, to this day remains a bit on the fuzzy side. There I had my head wound cleaned which by then was becoming quite bad.

Thinking back, I should have received some medical attention for that, ideally a wee trip to A&E, but to an already half brain-dead teenager, at least that's what all the teachers used to say, it was a badge of honour.

The next morning came, and good God, my head was splitting, so, on top of my vodka hangover, always a good one, I had a gash the size of the Grand Canyon on top of my loaf of bread. Added to which, I still had to go home to listen to my mother shite on, 'why does your head looked like a bloody open coconut? Is it sore? Can I see it? What was I doing with my life?' You know, the usual mothering crap, but to someone on a come down with a bad, at this point, hangover.

Goddamn, what a way to start the year!

Now, what I didn't know, and at the time none of us did, was that this fight wasn't done yet. Not by a long shot. No. It would take another three weeks to find its ending with two smashed up homes and one family moving away.

The family in question being a bunch of hairy bikers that stayed just feet away from where it all began. Why they ran out that night for a ding dong I will never know. Maybe the hairy bikers celebrate New Year's different from the rest us; sing Auld Lang Syne, shake some hands, and kick some ass, who knows? What I do know is at some point during the day of January1st '98 word got back to the young team on the culprits behind all that shit from the previous night.

I can't say who was all there, and I doubt very much the police would care now, suffice to say that some of the guys involved that day still live in the area, and I wouldn't want to cause them any unwanted grief. Besides, everything I know is second hand. The only thing I know for sure is that about seven or more of the CYF went straight through their door smashing up the house as they went. They cornered and battered four guys in the living room while the other three jumped out the window and took to their heels to places unknown.

All the boys involved probably thought to themselves 'fuck it job done. Nothing more to worry here. Just another bit of good old fashioned street violence with no repercussions.'

They were wrong, very wrong.

Less than a week later. We were all back doing what we did best, drinking and dropping E's in Tony Docherty's house. We had been in his home over a dozen times before with nothing major ever happening. Maybe a spilled drink or broken glass, but that was about it. Not that night though, that night would be different. At some point in the early morning, just after dawn, I was sleeping lightly having called it a night an hour so before.

There was a loud bang, bang, bang at the door. My first thought without a doubt, was that it must be the police or polis as they're called in and around the Glasgow area. This was different I don't know why, a gut feeling maybe told me something's wrong here.

Even from the third level of the home in a bedroom with the door closed, I knew that the banging was the sound of trouble. My intuition turned out to be spot on. (If only that shit would work every time I visit my bookie, but sadly not.)

So anyway, back to that night. Accompanying the bangs came shouting with threats of violence. Suddenly I was wide awake, something was very badly wrong.

Out of nowhere came Kev Williamson doing his impression of Jack Flash. Like a bullet he went flying past me shouting, 'That mob from last week are downstairs, tooled up mate and looking for everyone involved with smashing up their house. Fucking run, Paul!' No sooner had he said that he's up the loft hatch. And, to make matters worse, he fucking closes the hatch leaving me standing stunned with disbelief, fucking rascal that he was. So my only other option was out the window. Three levels up. *Fuck it why not,* I think to myself.

So there I am, around 7am, doing my Spiderman impression down a drainpipe, hanging on to the outside of the building for dear life.

I get to the second level, the Livingroom window to be more precise. When this fat cocksucker sees me and flings a hatchet, a fucking hatchet, (I mean come on mate, you should see someone about that temper,) at the window I'm just about gripping onto. *Fuck you* I think to myself as I let go and fall to the garden below. It wasn't the highest of heights and certainly a better bet than what was heading my way only a few seconds before. The irony of it was fat boys fling was worse than his weight. It never even scratched the glass.

Anyway, fuck that and fuck you tubby I was off taking to the hills hoping no one was behind Me?

I later found out that they all more of less just left without incident. After that the old paranoia started to set in. Was it me that they had been there for the whole time? Did all that kick off last week as ruse just to get at me? Who the fuck were these people? Why were they after little old me? I never did find out who they were. Thankfully they moved a few days later and I've never heard from them since and doubt I ever will.

At the same time all this was going on I was running around with another group. One night in Millcroft with everyone down there the other day/nights with Andy McKinnon and his crew.

Now, Andy was a great guy. And a lot of fun to be around. He was also mad about stealing motorbikes and for some reason Cumbernauld at the time was going through a moped craze. Perfect for us. There wasn't a week went by we weren't out stealing them.

It wasn't hard to do. All you needed was some bolt-cutters and to be fast on your feet and you were off. Believe me when I tell you, we tried to steal every one of them. I don't think there was a housing scheme in this town we didn't go into at one point and robbed it blind and not just mopeds, everything we could get our hands on.

Now Graham stark aka Starky was the real brains behind it. He came from a family of auto mechanics and was around engines all his life. So, starting up a moped without any keys was just another day at the office, easy-peasy lemon-squeezy. So that was our new thing. For a while we even had old, abandoned, garages that we cut the padlocks off and replaced them by putting our own new ones on. We kept the mopeds in there, out the way of prying eyes.

It's fair to say, the Carbrain area was always a crime ridden scheme. Even here you always had one or two noisy neighbours with the police on speed dial. The safest option was to just to keep them out of sight.

We weren't running a chop shop nothing like that just taking them and riding them all over town until they broke, or the polis found them. Funny thing was, we only ever got chased on them a few times.

One thing that always stands out in my mind came at around the end of that summer. We were down in a factory area in the bottom end of Cumbernauld next to the train station kicking the shit out of this moped when Andy says, 'Jump on Paul.' So, with him driving and me on the back flying up the road, the hot sun on our backs, it was heaven for a second anyway. As we were heading back down the long road, we came face to face with a police car. The best thing about it. Their reasoning for being down had nothing, whatsoever to do with us. Just a male and female officer down in a back road, out the way, in a rundown factory area. Well, I'll let you decide what they were there for.

Oops sorry guys, but it's looking like no fucky-fucky-fuck-fuck for yous today. Of course, there is absolutely no proof that this was going on but it's still a fun thought to think and anytime I drift back to that day in my mind's eye it always makes me laugh.

So, there we were, two daft wee tits on an overpowered hair dryer heading straight at them. They hit the lights and made some sounds with their siren, the driver no doubt thinking to himself, I'm getting these wee wankers, and I might even look the big man in front of my side kick by cuffing them and taking them down hard.

Now Andy was heading right at them and I'm on the back thinking, *'does this fucking maniac think we are riding a Kangaroo. How the hell are we supposed to jump over this bloody car?'* When out of nowhere, and I must give him credit for this, he takes a left onto the path and right around the shocked looking officers.

There's a bang and a thud as we came back off the curb and onto the road again. Realising the gravity of the situation we knew we had to get our skates on and take off like a rocket, using the vital seconds it took them to turn their car around to make our sharp get away. In no time, they were right on our tail, lights and sirens going mad. I mean, they were going the full ten yards trying to catch up with us, but fortune was to favour us on that occasion. I remember thinking, *'Sorry guys but today is just not going to be your day,'* as we hit the slip path up towards the Bell's shop and off into the mist.

By now though, even before our wee chase, they had us well and truly in their sights. Not that we had any idea or even cared. Stealing motorbikes was far from the only thing we were up to back then.

One of our favourite pastimes was robbing the catalogue vans as they made their deliveries to the old tenement blocks. These were big, long maisonette style blocks known locally as the verandas.

We would hide behind a big red brick wall while one boy would stand on the long pathway running across the flats and watch if the delivery guy went right to the end or the middle. Then we would run over, and someone would screw the lock back. Back then the locks to the vans were bullshit, daft locks that anyone who knew anything about them could break within seconds. Having gained entry, we would jump in the back like a bunch of Jackals, grab as many boxes, sealed bags, and everything else lying there we could, and run off before the delivery guy came back to find that his van had been screwed.

We honestly never considered the poor driver might lose their job over it. I mean I hope no one ever did, that one wouldn't have sat right with me. Bottom line, I came from, no, let me rephrase that, I come from working class people and I would have carried a lot of guilt for that one.

Anyway, these wee turns were never supposed to last long, we all knew that much even at fourteen-fifteen years old. For us it was a case of get as much as you can as fast as you can. Then move on. The good times never last.

Before long the delivery vans started coming down the street accompanied by, you guessed it, the Police. So, we knew right there and then it was done and dusted. No big deal. Most of these actions were done out of pure boredom. Making a few dollars from it was just a plus.

On top of the day-to-day crime, we were witnessing within our area things like people openly selling smack on the streets. People arriving in stolen cars, heroin dependent people, shoplifting and coming to our doors to sell things to our mothers and fathers, we always loved that. It was like Christmas in July watching them go door-to-door with bags of what they got that day. Some of them were right good at it too. They'd go up the local shopping centre, known to the natives as the toonie, with lists from would-be bargain hunters. I don't think I ever saw David Dickinson down there, but who knows?

Of course, these buyers were mostly woman with their man occasionally coming down to the door maybe to try something on or pay them for their bag of goodies. None of them ever thought what they were doing was breaking the law, just getting stuff for cheap, and why not? In my opinion life's hard enough without the worry of not having enough money to get the things your kids need.

When they came over with something good, all the women in the scheme were out looking for a bargain, most were on the dole or single parents just trying to get by. A wee brucie-bonus for someone sitting on hard times. Safe to say, most of the people we knew fell into that category.

The only thing we never saw much of was violence of a savage nature. There was violence no doubt, we saw that on an almost daily basis, but real, life-threating stuff, not so much. Or, if it was there, I was still to sheltered from most of it. More street fights, people getting bottled, things like that.

The first murder I ever heard about happened in the winter of that year. A pub fight gone bad, the victim, a man by the name of Andrew Healy. I don't know what the exact ins and outs of this fight were, but I heard tell, it all happened over a boy who had had far too much to drink. He didn't realise just how much of a pest he was becoming, constantly going over to customers, annoying them and more. He repeatedly went up to Big Tam Hunter pestering him, and Big Tam was beginning to take the bite, getting visibly agitated; then something stupid was said. Sometimes that's all it takes.

A fight broke out with Tam pulling a lock back knife and stabbing him in the stomach. Now a few things went against this Healy guy that night. The first thing was him getting caught in the cross hairs of the polis to begin with and, number two, Tam stabbed him that fast he never even noticed.

Now people may be thinking how you can get stabbed and not notice? Well, anyone unlucky enough to have this happen to them will tell you, a stab wound to the abdomen can feel like nothing more than a punch to the stomach. A bit like getting winded and I'm guessing that's what might have happened here.

The third thing to play its part that night was by far the worst. Healy's friend thinking that the fight was over with no real bad outcome took his friend home putting him on the coach to sleep it off. Only to find his mate dead the following morning. The poor guy bled out there and then. If someone had only noticed any one of those three things, the guy might still be here today but, unfortunately, fate had other plans.

The next morning the news broke with the jungle drums beating loudly. By the afternoon everyone knew who was responsible. At the time, the name Tam Hunter was unknown to me. I had heard his name from my uncle, but I never knew the man. All I knew was the police were hot on his trail and the pub had men and women with white suits and brown evidence bags going in, out, and all around it all day.

Tam was eventually caught and sentenced to twelve years, of which he probably served seven or eight, but not before a half dozen doors were kicked in from overzealous police officers in their hunt for fat Tam.

I say overzealous because on one of their many outings they almost put me flat on my arse running up the block of flats I was staying in at the time. They hit my neighbour's door; best thing about it was that they were a couple of squares and had nothing to do with anything. Talk about bad intelligence, poor guys had their house turned upside down at the crack of dawn on a Saturday morning. What a wakeup call that must have been.

As for me, I had been sent for the morning paper and milk on my bike, nothing new here. Saturday morning milk runs had become part of my weekend routine. Which had all started from my days working on the milk vans where I would bring home a few pints at the end of my shift.

Only this Saturday would be anything but routine. I had just put my hand on the door of the thick, heavy close when, from the other side, two fat very eager to go boys of the blue shield came crashing through the other side knocking me flat on my behind looking up from the dirty floor of the Millcroft flat.

I got to witness what can only be described as something straight out of a Keystone Cops sketch as I went flying one way, my bike went another, and like a human choo-choo, there followed over a half dozen of them barging through the door and crash, they were all sent flying over my bike and into the air. Before I could even think of apologising, this big mean looking bastard barked back at me. 'Get that fucking bike out the way you little prick. Now, before I put your head through the wall.'

I was stunned, I mean *they* knocked me down. Later that day I came to realise the truth. They had not one but two female colleagues with them and I must have made them look like morons. It was a complete accident. One thing's for sure, it was just another reason I had to add to my already growing hatred of all thing's *authority*. I unfortunately carried this with me most of my life, even today I struggle with being told what to do. Not the best quality to have when you're a chef.

I can't in all good faith sit here and say that one moment turned me against the system. No, that honour lies mostly with my schoolteachers who hardly took a moment to think or notice that this boy might be struggling with the work they were handing out.

It was easier for them to label me a fuck-up and wash their hands of me. You see the same stuff happening even today, nothing more but the same old story, 'that kid is a fuck up put them to the back of the class and let's get on with the lesson.'

This was the same year John Duncan got stabbed. John was one the funniest people you could ever be around at this point and time. We never knew each other but you always heard the stories about him and the mad shit he got up too. I'm telling you, some of the tales told about him would have had you on the floor laughing with tears in your eyes.

Unfortunately, one Saturday morning everyone in Carbrain came to know the name John Duncan. He was the boy who got Butchered the night before. *Fuck me*, I thought on hearing this. I had heard of the guy through the folk I ran with. This wasn't a couple of guys I had never heard of before. I had seen him kicking about, even spoken with him a few times, and now this.

And when I say he got butchered he did, to this day it's still only the second worst stabbing I've ever known about. The number one spot belongs to someone we will get to later in the book.

Like I said, I was jumping in between two groups of friends and one day Cumbernauld was awoken with the story from the night before of a boy, aged just 16, that had been stabbed. It was a bad one from the way the jungle drums of Cumbernauld were beating.

That boy, John Duncan, got stabbed in the stomach and the word around the campfire was that his guts were hanging out of the open wound. I remember standing there listening to my friends' rabbit on about what they knew or what they had heard about the events that had escalated the night before. All I had to do was imagine what state he must have been and how he walked through four streets holding his insides in his hands. In my mind I'm thinking *'bullshit, no one could ever survive that either he's dead or it was never as bad as it's getting made out to be.'*

How wrong I was. It turned out he did in fact walk all that way and, even more shockingly, he did so with his insides out. Now the details the of this story are not mine to tell, plus the telling of such could potentially open an old wound for lack of a better word, so all I will say on this is, I for one am very glad that John never died that night as the world would have lost one of its best.

Of course, John and I would become inseparable over the years to come, with some of my finest memory's owed to him and all his madness. He was a great guy to be around back then.

1998 didn't just see John getting stabbed but I popped my cherry that year too, along with almost stabbing a man to death, getting charged and walking on a technicality. Here I can only provide vague details but not the injured guy's name. This is largely due to the fact I honestly can't remember it. What I do remember of that day is this:

It was the Summer of 98, one of those real hot summers. And that day was over the top hot. So hot the shopping centre had to open its fire exits - which also served as the loading bays for the shops to take in stock. Good for keeping the staff cool, even better for a bunch of thieving little bastards like us.

We had already been inside the shopping centre that day and been followed around by every security guard this side of the Mississippi. So, we thought *fuck it, let's head out of here and come back in an hour or so and try our luck then.*

Now, going out the back way of the building is something we wouldn't normally do as it takes you out in the opposite direction to where we wanted to go. Who knows why we changed our minds and started walking out the back exits instead of the front, maybe the Gods were shining down on us that afternoon, who knows. Whatever the reason, we found ourselves

looking down an almost endless row of unmanned exits to all the shops storerooms. Jack pot! We went from shop to shop, grabbing as much as our arms could handle before making our exit. As we ran off, we couldn't help but giggle, delirious with excitement. We ran until eventually we got to an underpass far enough away where we felt safe. No one was on our trail.

We looked over it all, a damned good day's work to say the least. Then it was 'Right Lads, let's get down to Milcroft and start turning this into cash money. I think it took just under an hour and the full load was gone and all of us sitting pretty. Extreme heat and pockets full of money not the best recipe for a peaceful day. You know temptation is always the strongest voice in the room, so the decision was made: 'Fuck it boys, let's get pissed.'

We started the afternoon off with one bottle of Buckfast each, then two, then more to follow. Probably not the smartest thing to be doing in that heat. Einstein's we were not. By three o clock we are all flat out drunk with not a sensible word between us. Then one of us decided, I'm not sure who, 'Let's got down to Greenfaulds for a good old gang fight.'

To this day I don't know why any of us thought it was a good idea. None of us could stand straight on our feet let alone fight. We all thought, yes what a brilliant idea, let's go down there and get stuck right into this mob.

Hard as I try, I can't even remember the walk down there that day or much about the build- up to the fight in question. Thinking back, it was one of those things where you find yourself smack-bang right in the middle of it.

It was around teatime, just as the sun was starting to set, when three guys turned the corner. They were just right there as we were on our way back to our own turf. They started shouting at us. *Fuck me* I thought, here we go.

My mate Scott was first in as usual, nothing new there. Now Scott was a quite stoner; a Dr Who type Motherfucker but, credit where it's due, when it came to going ahead, he had balls bigger than an orangutan's ass, and the rest of us were right at his back.

As the ding-dong turned into a full-scale brawl, some random guy, for whatever the reason I honestly don't know, thought he could just stroll right through the middle of it. I can't think what was in this guy's mind or why he thought he could walk through this madness and come out the other side unharmed. He must have been on the run from the Rubber Room no doubt. Anyway, long story short I see him walking straight towards me. The yellow handled lock back I had on me found its way into my hand, the knife part opened and pointed outwards. Bang, bang, bang, before I knew what was happening, he had been stabbed.

Then everything went quiet.

All the shouting and screaming of everyone knocking fuck out of each other dissolved away. Once I realised, he was stabbed all the commotion and noise of the fight came flooding back. Then, I heard someone shouting, 'Fuck me, Paul has just stabbed the fuck out of him. Let's get the hell out of here.'

I looked down to see this boy lying buckled on the ground. The knife was still in my hand with his blood staining not only the lockback but my Lacoste tracksuit and white trainers which were badly splattered and not only looked unfit to wear but also very indictable.

The shock hit me like a tidal wave. I was rooted to the spot trying to compute what had happened then I heard someone say:

'Right guys, time to disappear.' We realised that all the commotion this would cause was bound to have knock on effects and draw some negative attention. We knew the drill, we had been there multiple times before and knew the police were heading to the scene.

HEADING FOR THE BIG LEAGUE

Everyone broke up from what can only be described as a deadly looking scrum. Our side taking off together, heading back to HQ and safer pastures.

What happened to the other boys is a question lost to time. Who knows? What I do know is: within two hours Strathclyde Police intel had all five of our names, addresses and knew where we hung out.

Me and Scott were first to be apprehended. They grabbed Scott while he was waiting on me coming out a shop, at this point they never knew I was inside.

I watched Scott being detained on the shop's CCTV system. The shop's camera was set up so you could see all the camera angles from the big TV mounted on the ceiling. So, there I was crouching down behind the tins of dogmeat peeking up at the monitor praying like mad they didn't walk in.

The shopkeeper was no doubt thinking is he shoplifting dogfood or just so hungry that he's getting stuck into a few tins of pedigree chum, either way I want this crackpot out my store as soon as possible.

As I watched the cuffs go on Scott, I was thinking to myself, are they leaving? Am I in the clear here? Then, one eagle-eyed bobby thinks *why not pop my head into Jazz's shop, maybe I'll find more of the five neds we're hunting. Or maybe I'll catch a 14-year-old peeking out from behind the pedigree chum.* Whatever his reasoning, the jig was up.

I was promptly arrested and taken to the station for questioning along with Scott. Given both of us were under the age of sixteen we could only be interviewed with an appropriate adult. Now, this was around 9pm and unfortunately for the CID conducting the interview it fell on the same night that my mother, Angie, stepfather and uncles were having a Smith family shindig. Along comes Angie, pissed as a poet on payday and wanting to come in on the interview. God, I wish I had the transcripts from that night.

She demanded to see the witness statements and buoyed up with alcohol proceeded to tell them, 'The only things yous cunts how to do right is bully kids. My boy is innocent of any shit you bastards are throwing at him. Yous have him in here with this shite when you should out be catching bank robbers and paedophiles.'

I remember thinking bank robbers and paedophiles. What an odd pair, but there you go.

No sooner had I heard that when a polis personnel started telling my mother, 'You shut your mouth!' Needless to say, the exchanges got more heated, and she replied, 'Why don't you tell your wife to shut her legs your friends are getting bored.' Normally my mother is so shy when it comes to that sort of talk. To this day she makes me apologise if I say the word cunt in her company. So, for her to hit out with that was game changing!

That Vodka had got a lot to answer for but that was her in a nutshell. A small woman with a vehement *not-my-boy* attitude, though the look on the polis' face was almost worth the five hundred years he was looking to give me.

At this point the cavalry arrived in the guise of my lawyer. I was 14 years old and in that much trouble the police had advised that I should have a lawyer present as this was not going to the Children's Panel.

'No my boy, this is going the Sheriff Court and with any luck maybe even the High Court.'

So, sticking with who you know, my family called David Hall of Hall & Haughey solicitors. Davie was the only choice. He had already successfully defended some members of my family for various minor misdemeanors throughout the years. So, you can understand why he was the number to call.

This was my first time ever meeting him. He was a fat, bald guy with a hard look on his face. The first words out his month were, 'Remember you have the right to say no comment Paul,' not even a hello, just straight to the point. I now know that was him telling me in no uncertain terms, keep your mouth shut. It's your right to do so. Though even I knew at that point there wasn't anything he could have done to help me. Even Johnnie Cochran, defence attorney for O J Simpson could not have got me home on this.

I had been named, they had the knife, they had CCTV from that day and a few statements against me. They had more information than the internet and of course, the only thing left was to hammer that last nail into my coffin; the identification parade. Five witnesses came in and all five picked me out, one after the other. Then Scott went five for five directly after me. Then Graham and Russell were picked out once each and Ginger unsurprisingly got picked out from the carpark with that bright red hair of his. Poor boy, he never stood a chance. Why he never dyed or even shaved that nut of his I will never understand. He was always one of the first to get grabbed by the polis; a trend that follows him to this day.

We were all arrested and charged. Our age meant that we couldn't be detained overnight so Russell and I were released overnight on police bail. We were ordered to report to the station the following morning at 8am sharp with a warning: if you run, we will badger your homes, harass your family and friends, and scorch the earth to find you.

At the time I felt notorious, like I was stepping out of the shadows and into what I thought was the big league with all the glamour and status that came with it. How wrong I was. I had no concept of what was heading my way or how far I was going to fall.

The next morning came, and I was up like a shot getting ready. Then around 7.45am my mother accompanied me on the short walk up to then police station. It was only a few streets away from our house. The sun was just coming up at our backs, hitting the damp grass and filling the air with that fresh cut-grass smell. To me it's the best part of the day and always a good time to let your mind just drift. It wasn't long before my mind began to ponder all the negative possibilities of what lay ahead. I wasn't daft, I knew we were in for a significant punishment and rightly so. Even in my young teenage years I understood there were just some things in life where you needed to just accept the consequences. This was definitely one of those times.

My thinking at the time was bravado bullshit, my aims that year centred on wanting to pop my cherry and getting locked up for the first time. However, when it comes and you're standing on the edge looking into the abyss it's still a scary place to be.

By the time we arrived at the copshop the consequences that lay before me stood out starkly. I was nervous, my mouth dry but at the same time my heart drummed with excitement. I could see my mother was anxious, she was quiet, her face etched with concern and disappointment.

Finally, we walked through the station doors. The CID were already standing waiting on us.

'Right Paul come with us.'

A door was held open for me to walk through when just at that moment my lawyer appeared, he pulled me to one side and said in no uncertain terms, 'No matter what gets said in there, your reply will be 'No Comment' and nothing more. Do you understand?'

'Yes.'

The interview stage was very uneventful. Just a battery of questions going round and round in an attempt to get me to open my mouth, catch me out and sink myself. Even back then I knew the rules. We were brought up with this shit happening all around us. Going in and out of interviews was just something we had to deal with. It was part and parcel of a life we thought we wanted.

I often think of that boy that was stabbed and wonder if he ever had any lasting damage. I hope not as that was one of my biggest regrets. My actions that day made me feel sick to my stomach and haunts me even to this day.

We were Neds, not animals and young Neds at that, most of us averaging the age of fourteen. What we lacked in foresight and maturity we made up for with impulsiveness and a skewed sense of bravado. The boy got caught up in a gang fight and was injured badly. He gave a statement against all of us granted, but that doesn't mean I wish the boy any ill will. I truly hope he has moved on with his life and today is a happy man.

As the seasons changed from autumn to winter the trial date finally came upon us. November 2nd, Court One, Airdrie Sheriff Court. There we were five fuckups acting like we were Billy Big Balls.

I was the second youngest, a small and skinny lad sitting on the dock. My legs didn't even make it all the way to the floor.

The court wasn't exactly what I was expecting. My understanding of how it worked was informed by watching tv with all the flash and drama of the courtroom portrayed in those scenes. In my head I had conjured images of these big dramatic trials, lawyers arguing back and forth, the judge sitting in stern deliberation and all ending with a load of verdicts of 'not guilty' echoing around the room. How wrong I was. In a strange way I felt disappointed, we had no opportunity to speak, there was a lot of paper shuffling and long silences as clerks and lawyers exchanged papers and whispers while we the accused sat in silence, totally bored, and not fully understanding the process.

Over a long period there was a lot of going back and forth to the court while the lawyers wrangled and debated, all before the first witness had been called.

Then one day, Sheriff Dickson stopped the trial for a ten-minute recess with all the lawyers looking pretty happy with themselves.

We, the accused were totally unaware of what was about to happen. The first witness would have been taking the stand that day but for the Judge suddenly announcing that the case was to be thrown out because of a time bar technicality. We had gone over the one year one day caveat which in Scotland means that your lawyer can appeal to have your case thrown out. This is what happened to us.

Looking back, I'm convinced now that had I been sent down then I doubt I would have followed the reckless path I did. In all honesty, my heart wasn't in following that lifestyle, I just got swept up by it and carried along. I wasn't mature enough to consider the consequences, the saying that youth is impulsive is true, certainly in my case.

STEPPING INTO THE WORLD OF DRUGS

With the '90s in the rear-view mirror, we all stepped into not only a brand-new millennium but also, for most of us, a big fork in the road of life. Most of the young team broke up; some went into full-time work, others went to college, and some guys even started looking at beginning brand-new lives altogether with their lifelong partners by their side. And why not? They were, without a doubt, the smartest ones among us.

With most of the young team now turning sixteen, only myself and John McMillan, still fifteen, felt left out. Not realizing the benefits of still being a minor - that was my attitude. I was always trying to race through life, always wanting to hit the important milestones, never wanting to slow down to catch a breath, not appreciating the best part of still being underage in the eyes of the law.

The best thing about being underage was, of course, getting detained by the police. By now it happened almost daily. It didn't matter to them if you had done anything or not. They would do a stop and search, and if that turned up negative, they would hit you with a breach of peace charge. Because I was still under the age of sixteen, I was usually out within six hours. Just a quick scolding from your mother, and you're back with your friends before your Buckfast even gets warm.

Now, the smart ones of the group are beginning to realise that the way we were all fooling around was totally bullshit, and it was time to start making some serious changes.

As for the rest of us, well, we were doing what we always did: thieving, fornicating, and fighting.

And, of course, when the weekends came, everyone still got together for yet another episode of "This is your life," Ned style.

My weekends would always start at a girl's house who, at the time, was extremely close to me. I mean, she was like a sister to me; that's how close we were back then. She is a real member of my family, just not my sister.

However, she has asked that I keep her name anonymous so, for the sake of her privacy, I will refer to her from now on as 'Jelly.'

The weekends could only ever start in one place for me: Jelly's home and no other. And it would always start the same way, with a bottle of Buckfast and a couple of ecstasy tablets, and even a wee ten deck of Club Ks in the back pocket. No matter where it ended, it always started there.

I had been going to Jelly's home for a few years now but, by this stage, I was probably at her home four days a week and out of my nut for at least three of those days. She must have had a trusting face because my mother never questioned why I would disappear on Friday afternoon, usually not coming home until Sunday breakfast time, unless, of course, the police caught up with me and I spent the weekend in the cells.

Some of my best times were within Jelly's four walls. One occasion that comes to mind was on the fourth day of a five-day bender. I had been going at it hard, I mean hard. When I started to hit the trip stage of my MDMA roller-coaster ride, I turned to Jelly and asked her, "Do you like that telly?" She stood there, looking back at me with a "What the fuck are you talking about, you fucking space cadet?" expression on her face. I continued to babble; I told her to keep an eye out for any store security. "Paul, what the fuck are you talking about?" she asked, starting to realise how high I must have been.

In my ecstasy-induced madness, I must have thought I was in a shop, not Jelly's living room. So, there I was, standing in her living room, attempting to unplug her TV. To make matters even funnier, in the presence of numerous other people in her home, I started taking down my tracksuit bottoms, thinking I was going to stuff the TV down one of my legs. Mind you, this was a television from the '90s when flat screens were still science fiction. God knows how I thought I would fit it down my leg, let alone what I was planning to do if I ever managed to get out with it.

As you can imagine, Jelly's TV remained plugged in, and everyone erupted with laughter, especially Jelly. She knew better than most that I was completely out of it that day. I was told to shut up and sit down, Honestly, the stick I had to endure for that incident went on for weeks, all in good fun of course. That was just one of the many times ecstasy played a big part in fucking up my life, sometimes in the funniest of ways, sometimes in mad ways, and sometimes in bad ways.

Probably the worst experience for me on those little white pills was back in the '90s. It was only the second time I had ever taken one. This brand (commonly known as Mitzi) must have had a very high level of MDMA in it.

You see, the problem with ecstasy is you never quite know how much MDMA, or amphetamine is in them. If you're lucky, you get one that's only mixed with the correct amount.

The problem, of course, is greed. The more popular the drug becomes, the more likely people are to start mixing it with cheaper, more deadly substances to maximize profits. Obviously, no one wants to kill anyone. That's bad for business.

If you do get a deadly one, it's never personal, just some clown who couldn't mix a drink, let alone lethal pills.

The fact of the matter is, as long as you stay alive, it means you're 'out there' weekend after weekend buying more and more. Pure capitalism at its best. It was bad luck for me on that particular weekend. The pills going around had enough ketamine in them to kill Shergar. I don't even believe they had any MDMA in them.

So, off I went down to the off-sales to find a loose-minded adult who had no qualms buying nine or ten bottles of Scotland's other national drink, Buckfast; a black sweetened wine made in Devon and sold in every corner shop on our side of the border.

From there, I went back up to our area to buy the drugs. This was a lot easier and faster to obtain than the Buckfast from the shop only two streets away. It was just the sad fact of life where we lived at the time. On average every Friday night, you could stand in one spot, do a three hundred and sixty degree turn and see six different people selling six different kinds of drugs. Sometimes, and I may be embellishing a bit here, down to a small boy selling you everything you needed to fuck yourself right on your very doorstep.

The police, or to be more precise, the drug squad, would occasionally come down and do a round-up, but they never caught anyone above street level. Even if they did catch them, they didn't make a dent on the so-called war on drugs. Not that we wanted them to catch anyone - the smack trade maybe, but that was it. We all loved the fact that you could get hash, ectos and LSD as fast as getting a double nugget from the ice cream van.

But, like I said, the pills were getting mixed more and more with bad reports coming out almost every weekend.

BAD TRIPS

Finally, it was my turn to experience the bad side of the drugs

I dropped my pill just like before with a vague awareness of what was ahead of me.

Or I thought I did.

Ten minutes or so went by, and the tingles started. Only these were faster and stronger than before. Tingles rushing up from my toes; that warm almost hot feeling flooding over me with the 'I love everybody and everything, I just love, love, urge taking over.

Everything so far was so good then bang, suddenly I go into fifth gear. The boot goes down and I was totally out of control. The tingles coming faster and stronger than I had ever felt before.

When I think about it even in the very beginning of the rushes, I knew something was wrong. It was too strong, and I was quickly losing control.

Within fifteen minutes I was on the ground going into spasms. Thank God there were no empty bathtubs lying around, or my sick fuck mates would have had me in there, rolling in every direction. As I lay there, black eyes popping out my head and rolling every which way, my jaw was like an open office drawer and my teeth chattered so fast I was almost sending out morse code.

At that point you would think someone would have thought to call an ambulance, but no, all their sweeties had all been good ones. How that happened, who knows? Perhaps I also had a good one but was just too young and green behind the ears to handle it.

So, with the happy hardcore music blasting from the boombox, everyone else danced almost on top of me without a care in the world. They overlooked the fact that a boy was rocking and rolling on the ground at their feet. They were all as high as kites themselves, probably thinking to themselves, "Fuck me, Paul is off to see the wizard. That lucky bastard must have gotten the best of the bunch." Then, a boy who I will only call Tony, instead of giving me some chewing gum to stop me grinding my teeth, put a fucking lighter in my mouth instead.

Who the fuck thinks that's even a semi-intelligent idea is beyond me. How that lighter never exploded in my face, I will never understand. Thankfully, someone with at least one working brain cell took it out of my mouth and pulled out some Hubba Bubba. Only for Dr. Tony to step in. "I'll give it to him. I'll just put it in his mouth." It never worked out well for him.

From what I'm told, he stuck his big dirty finger and thumb with the chewy delight in between them into my mouth. Only for me to almost bite them off.

He screamed for help, "Someone get my fucking fingers out of his mouth before I lose them!" I continued to chomp on without a care in the world, while the others helped him avoid losing the tips of his fingers, at the very least.

I lay there, totally out of my banger, probably trying my hardest to come to terms with the fact that it was not the Hubba Bubba I was promised, but two big dirty digits that I was chomping down on.

Ah well, that's what he gets for being a smartass. Still, I am glad I never caused him any harm. This was still not the cherry on top, mind you. No, that came minutes later, with, as usual, with the arrival of Cumbernauld's finest.

Thankfully, by now, I had come down just enough to the point where I could at least see the world around me. The legs were still a bit shaky, though.

So, with the arrival of the boys in blue, rather than all the troops trying to run from the law with me weighing them down like a dead lump, these sick fucks gave me a leg and a wing right into a thornbush. I landed on broken branches and half-drunken wine bottles. Not that I even noticed or remember to this day.

All these stories from that night came second hand from a bunch of hysterical teens. Now, I'm not big into miracles, but how these two police officers never saw a bunch of teens high as the Himalayas catapult their comrade into a bush before taking off running with screams of laughter, I will never know.

Perhaps they just thought, "Sod that! All the paperwork we would have to do on this carry on." Although I hope that's not the case no matter how lazy anyone is. Surely no one would leave a teen on the ledge of death because the paperwork would be a pain the backside. I guess I will never know.

Whatever the reason they both turned around got back in the car and drove off, only for my very own DIY medical team to come back and fish me out of the thorns. From there, I was taken down to Milcroft swing park and left lying on a park bench to come back down to earth. "Ground control to Major Tom" suddenly started to make sense on almost every level.

At last, my mind found my body, and finally, I started to move in sync. I could hold a cigarette in my hand, and even my eyes had begun to slow down enough to focus on my surroundings. My first images were of six of my amigos, all looking down at me from their ivory towers with a look of total disgust. Not because I came closer to death than any teen should. Not because they all didn't give a damn about me lying in a ditch. Not even because I was as filthy as fuck. Because I got higher than a giraffe's ass on the exact same pills, they all took themselves. Still, for all the bad that could have happened, a few *you should be ashamed of yourself* looks were far from the worst.

THE ISLE OF SKYE

That night, I was staying with Scott at the McKinnon household. The three of us were all going on a boys' holiday together to Skye, where the McKinnon family originally came from. The oldest brother, Andy, had already returned there a year or so earlier. Andy and I were always close, and I had been looking forward to seeing him for the past few weeks.

On the morning we were leaving, I had my first real come down, the drug equivalent of a hangover, only ten times worse. And that's before I even came to terms with the multiple ulcers burning inside my mouth. Ulcers, sweats, dry mouth, and paranoia—my brain felt like it was about to melt and pour out from my ears. All this and much, much more. All I could think about was the fact that we had a three-and-a-half-hour bus ride. So I thought there's only one thing for it: let's get drunk.

Even before Buchanan Street Bus Station, the three of us were at the back of our local bus, having vodka cocktails. Not quite a Tom Collins, more like straight into coke bottles. By the time our bus arrived, we were all so drunk that we were second-guessing ourselves—should we go?

We each had around £800 and two weeks to go mad anywhere we wanted without our parents knowing. Thankfully, Scott was the voice of reason, and finally, we boarded the bus for the long journey northbound. With the vodka beginning to sink in and the hangover finally starting to lift, I could concentrate more on the come-down part. Unfortunately, it was still killing me from the inside out, and the thought of being stuck on a bus with a bunch of strangers was intensifying my paranoia.

At this point, Scott came up with the idea of taking yet another one. "Right, troops, who's up for dropping another ecto each? Top of Form"

As his words vibrated in my ears, I thought to myself, "That's the fucking last thing I want to do." Then again, even just the thought of listening to the two of them sitting there, chewing their faces off, talking pure nonsense to one another sounded like absolute hell. What to do?

Fuck it, why not? The time was just after 10am on a Saturday morning, and here we were, three neds holding hands, skipping down the yellow brick road, so to speak, dropping ectos and drinking vodka. Not what you would call the breakfast of champions. In times of need, you would be surprised at what you would do just to feel better.

Thankfully, the bus ride zoomed past in the blink of an eye. Probably because we were all at the back of the bus with the ghetto blaster on low, laughing and joking, letting our hair down without the worry of facing Mum and Dad anytime soon.

Finally, we arrived at the Skye Bridge. Wow, I thought to myself, this place is stunning. I had been away before, my mother and stepfather taking us away a few times in my youth. I was also brought up in a grey concrete jungle, and it was very easy to forget just how beautiful our country was. It truly was something else.

Still, as much as we were up there to have fun, drink, do drugs and hopefully even engage in a little bit of fornicating (though I have to say, the only crabs I was planning on catching up there were from the shoreline, not the pantyline, if you get my drift). I must admit, the crabs you could eat up there were out of this world. Catching seafood like crabs, cockles, and my all-time favourite, king prawns, right from the sea and into the pot, there's nothing like it!

For boys like us growing up in Cumbernauld the closest any of us ever got to deep-sea fishing was maybe getting lost in the frozen aisle in Asda. I don't know if they would be cool with you breaking out the old fishing rod, maybe even getting a wee fire going. No, Asda might frown upon you for that one. It's a shame, though. I have only ever tasted that sort of freshness in a small handful of professional kitchens back in Glasgow. It has nothing to do with the restaurants not buying the best. Unfortunately, it's a race against the clock from the moment they come out of the big blue bath all the way onto your plate. The freshness is always dropping.

The local cuisine, of course, wasn't the only thing we had in our day planners. We were up there because we had been led to believe that the streets were paved with gold, and the poor folk who stayed there just didn't believe that there were thieving little shits like us in the world, let alone the small island they lived on. Come hell or high water, we were enroute to show them a lesson for not staying vigilant.

I can honestly say we never missed a building, even down to stealing the man's van who owned the campsites. Well, borrowed it anyway, so as we could go and break into the local supermarket.

You see, as nice as the island was, it was very rural. Everything was two or three miles away from each other. We had been in the store that day, clocking the place. It had an old-looking metal box they were using as a safe. It looked like a lockbox, small and not bolted to anything, with a big sign on it shouting at me and Apple Brandy (Andy), "Rob me, guys, for the love of God, rob me." Well, in our minds, the sign was there anyway. And like I've said before, me and Andy were the original two that started robbing everything in sight. So, if I was doing something from the pick of boys that happened to be there, it was without a doubt going to be with Apple Brandy. How could we get everything back to HQ? Forget just the box. Even if an alarm went off, who would ever hear it? Talk about the perfect rob. This one had us salivating, and we had only been there three days in the land of Skye. More like the land of fucking dreams. This was my Brinks Matt, and nothing was getting in my way.

So, me and Andy came up with the idea: let's wait until around 2am. The campsite owner, his dad I might add, was a drink-until-you-drop sort of guy.

So, the plan was simple: we steal his dad's car. Sod getting pinched before we even set out on the job, when the alternative was, we could just sit back and watch his dad getting rat-arse drunk. The idea being when he finally falls into his cot for the night, we can creep in, nab his keys, go down to the store, do what we came here to do, and be back before his morning hangover wakes him up. So, that's what we did.

While his dad watched the wee fat balding barman pour him pint after pint of thick black-coloured nectar, we watched him first starting to get happier and happier, and then sadder and sadder. Finally, around 11pm, he had his last round.

'Thank fuck,' Andy said, turning to me as we watched him stumble over towards the door. 'Come on, Dad, I'll get you home,' Andy grabbing him as best he could.

The pub was right at the site anyway, so we managed to get him into his caravan, thinking he's going to hit the sack right away. No, this big lump of a man starts cracking cans—one, two—then, finally on his third, the sandman came a-calling, and this big Viking-looking man-mountain hit the hay.

'Right, get the keys, and let's take the car for at least an hour. Don't want that big bastard waking up, catching us in the act.'

If I'm honest, I think I would just have run for home at that point. Never mind about the fact we were 230 miles away? Better taking the chance of making it home on foot.

So, there we were, back in our car, watching the clock- there is nothing worse than waiting to go out to commit any sort of crime. The longer you sit, the more likely you are to talk yourself out of doing it. I think Andy was the same, though he never said a word. He made some comments about *if he wakes up and we're out in his van, he will kill us.*

'Fuck it, the time has come. Let's get this done before we lose any more darkness.'

The scariest moment of that night wasn't the break-in or even the drive down. No, it was the reversing out of the small stone slab in front of his dad's caravan. The thought of him waking up was very nerve-racking. Still, we got it off the site without waking his dad or Scott or the other lad who went up for the wee break with us.

The drive down was very quiet, not much talking getting done, finally we got there, out the van and, as Andy worked on the back shutter with a Jack and pincher bar, I kept look out.

There came a loud crack and a bang as he got it up enough for us to start pulling at it. To my surprise it came away quite easy I guess it was old. Before we knew it, we were facing the fire exit door. Nothing special there just a normal thick door. Nothing a bit of brute force can't handle we figured and suddenly we were in the door. The alarm for some reason did not make a sound.

Could these people be that trusting that they don't even bother turning on the security system at night? Who knows? Perhaps it was old? Or perhaps they simply just forgot?

Whatever the reason we hit the jackpot as Andy worked on the door. I stood behind him, my adrenaline spiked to the point my hands were starting to shake. Then came a cracking of splintering wood and the back door gave way, and we were in right into the back storeroom. Nothing to write home about here, just a small room with some boxes and yet another door, thankfully it was unlocked.

As we ran through into the store, I started grabbing bottles of whisky and vodka. Andy kicked in the storeroom door behind the till where we hoped the small cash box and cigarettes were kept. I heard Andy's voice shout, "Jackpot. They're here," he ran past me, keeping grabbing stuff, and yelling.

I don't believe he meant to shout; I think it was just pure excitement that made him shout so loud as I ran frantically up and down like a contestant on Supermarket Sweep.

Before we knew it the car was full, and we were half wondering why we hadn't brought the van along. Still, not a bad day's work but we still had the job of getting back, unloading the car, and returning it.

By now the sun was coming up and bearing in mind this is farm-boy-country where their day starts around then. We knew we had better get moving. Thankfully we made it back to the site without incident and got everything out the car with only just one more thing to do - get the car back to the same spot it was last night and drop the keys in a manner that looked like he had dropped them in a drunken stumble.

Everything done. We crept back into the van that we were all sharing. Undressed and got into our beds. We both lay there not saying a word, but I was feeling like, did we honestly just get away with all of that? Then the paranoia kicked in.

You see, doing something you're not supposed to gives you a big hit of dopamine along with a very big adrenaline rush. These leave you with a feeling of euphoria and excitement, but unfortunately this comes with a cost. No sooner you come down from your natural high, the paranoia sets in, giving you in a way the same sort of feeling like the buyer's remorse - that moment when you totally regret doing something you just did only minutes before. As I lay there wrestling with my emotions the only real thing I could do is say to myself *what's done is done no point letting self-doubt set in now.*

Finally, we both fell asleep, only to be woken up by his dad at the caravan door. Thoughts of "Fuck, does he know?" raced through my mind, and from the look on Andy's face, he was thinking the same thing.

Scott opened the door. 'Alright, Dad,' to which his only reply was, 'Is Andy and the boy Paul in there?'

'Yes, they're here. Come in.'

At this point, I could almost hear my heartbeat in my ears, just waiting for him to go into a fit of rage. Turned out, he was there not to hand out ass whoopings, but only to ask if we had seen what he had done with his keys. His caravan was unlocked, so he must have let himself in, but he couldn't find them anywhere. Now, of course, we both knew exactly where they were, but we couldn't say anything.

'Aye, Andy,' (that's also the dad's name,) 'Someone will help you have a look for them.' If we had come out with, 'they're right beside the garden gnomes,' I think he would have smelled a rat with that one. So, we played dumb and told him we would help him look.

'Here they are,' seconds after getting to his caravan. 'You must have dropped them last night, ya pisshead.'

We all laughed at the same time, shooting a *thank-fuck-he-doesn't-know* look at each other.

Later that day, me and young Andy slipped away from everyone to go and burst open the lockbox. Not exactly millions in it, just £450 on top of the fags and booze. Not a bad day's work. We split the money and headed down to a shop that sold Buckfast, then back to the campsite to start getting fucked up.

The lack of sleep was starting to take its toll, and we had a choice: go to bed or take some pills and go down to the beach. No brainer there.

Scott, myself, Andy, and three other guys all headed down to the beach, half drunk and high as a motherfucker, and had a blast all day. Just daft young boys having fun and carrying on.

At some point during that day, Andy pulled me aside to say that he should be able to sell the fags and booze, but we had to keep very quiet about it. Fine by me. And that's basically what happened. Andy sold off the booze and most of the fags. We split the money, and for the rest of our time up there, we never spoke a word about it. Even when word started going around that the mini supermarket was broken into too, we simply acted daft, and as far as I know, no one was ever any the wiser.

A YEAR OF LIVING DANGEROUSLY (2000)

As far as affairs of the heart go, I had, by this point, hooked up with Nicola Wright, one of the most down-to-earth girls I have ever known. There was never any bullshit with her, just an all-around good person. Plus, she looked after my old man when I was living under government supervision, or to put it another way, serving time.

Back then, though, we were far from serious, just two young pups having fun until some fat arsehole, who the fuck even remembers, came out with the rumour that another girl was pregnant by me. Before I had the chance to speak with Nicole and tell her that the baby was not mine and I never ever even once put my babymaker anywhere near this girl, when boom, the rumour was ablaze. I mean, it was on every street corner out there. So, the truth made little difference by then. I would have even taken a fucking polygraph test. So, unless I am, in fact, God himself running around hitting females with the old immaculate conception trick, I can honestly say my conscience is clear, and that, my good people, is the truth.

It all came out as a made-up lie years later. By then, it made no difference. And what happened to me and Nicola, I hear you say? Well, no matter the truth or the lie, our time had come to an end.

Unfortunately, losing Nicola wasn't the only loss of the year 2000. We also lost a girl called Emma Cousins, a great wee lassie who, I'm sorry to write, took her own life by hanging herself in her home. I knew wee Emma quite a bit, as a matter of fact; we had our wee five-minute thing together, nothing heavy. I doubt most people even knew. And it was all over and done with for quite a while before she took her life.

I honestly don't know the real reason why she did what she did. And to be honest, I wouldn't write on it even if I did. I only know it hurt all of us bad. Our grief was nothing compared to the hurt felt by the girls of the group; they truly went through hell on that one. Emma's death affected them; it hit each one of them hard. She was, after all, CYF and one hundred percent one of the troops. Without a shadow of a doubt, we all were left with a heavy heart with her passing.

Sadly, this wasn't our only suicide that year; we also lost another mate just a few months later. And this one not only hit our wee gang hard but rippled through three different schemes. It was the death, or to be more precise, the suicide of wee William Paterson. The ins and outs of this one are still hard to write about some twenty-two years later.

If I'm perfectly honest, it was the only time I had any real reason to hate that mob from Abronhill. They came down to our scheme in the dead of night just after he hung himself and wrote mean, hurtful things on the walls of Glenhove shop about his death. That, in my opinion, showed bad form, but I guess that's life. I'm sure that now as an adult, he or they will no doubt feel rotten inside about that one.

Anyway, going back to the day we all found out, now that was a sad day. I still recall who told me, a boy called Nugget, he was standing just outside Carbrain Primary School football pitch. I stood there, looking down at the red ash of the old pitch, thinking how the heck can this be true? I had been kicking about with him only the night before as he sat sucking down on a bit of paper soaked in LSD, giggling away to himself as he told me about a turn he had planned and that if I wanted in. We were to meet up early the next day to pull it off and now this. What a terrible blow.

I couldn't take it in. I was sure Nugget must have been mistaken on this one. I ran over the bridge to his home turf to see for myself. My mind raced, and I wondered if John McMillan knew; he was, after all, one of his best mates. Though no one came closer to William P than that of William McCauley; those two changed one another's nappies as nippers.

A million thoughts flooded my mind then, without even realizing it I found myself standing at the bottom of Tarbolton Road, and who was standing right there but William McCauley. As he turned, the look on his face said everything. We just stood there, tears running down both our faces, not a word was spoken.

There could be no getting away from it; our friend, one of the troops and a great wee guy, was gone. It was hard to take in how someone so young with so much life ahead of him should suddenly decide to opt out.

I had once before felt the hollowness of losing someone to suicide, a cousin, but to be honest, we hardly knew each other. The impact of his death hit our family hard, but out of respect to his immediate family, I will not discuss this further. Wee Willy Patterson's death was a different kind of hurt; we had all been running together daily at this point, and it hit home in a way I had never felt before.

Then there was wee Kathy McGowan; she was his on-again, off-again girlfriend. My heart went out to her. I saw her in his mum's house the first night we all found out. She knew the wee man was in love with another girl but crushed on him hard nonetheless and truly looked broken that night. He also had a brother, Robert, who was at the time giving his own pound of flesh to the government, serving a sentence on some small-time bit; for who knows what, though unlike the life sentence he is now serving, he was due out not long after the funeral. So, while William's mum had his sister, and his sister had her, poor Robert had nothing but cinderblocks and noisy halls for comfort. I always remember thinking that poor guy must be going mad in there. I will say one thing though, I saw him at the funeral. And if he was pulling out his hair, he held that shit well. Even at the graveside, as he lowered his brother into the ground, a single tear ran down his face; he held it together like a real man. We all spoke about it afterward, and the feeling then was simple; there stood a man's man.

As for the rest of us, that was probably one of the hardest burials I have ever attended. The screams alone that came from his mother I'll never forget. I can still hear it in my mind's eye, still see her falling to the ground by his grave. It's weird; the small little details that stay with you.

Now and then, I still see Sandra, bump into her at the shop and the like. I never knew her before any of this, but I would be shocked if I found out that it never changed anything about her personality. I know that for anyone else who has suffered the loss of a child at sixteen, you never see them full of the same fun and laughter they had before.

As you can imagine, losing two mates in a few short months of one another put a dent in the lads' morale. We all stuck together best we could, but you could almost see the writing on the wall. Bit by bit everyone was starting to peel away. Me, John, Gary, Bryson, Humbug, my mate KitKat, and a few more began running about almost full time in Jelly's house. Milcroft seemed to have lost its appeal.

Darren Mills, Nicky Stevenson, wee Russell, and a few more who stayed down Milcroft way remained there. Our team was already shaved down to the bone and in time became almost halved. It was claimed that I split from my young team, and yes, in a lot of ways, I did. At that point, Carbrain had split up into a million different cliques anyway. Sometimes I travelled all the way from Seafar to Milcroft just for them all to be in the McKinnon house and blank the door when I chapped.

By this point Scott McKinnon had returned to Skye to live full time The point being, the old days were gone; it was time to start looking elsewhere for new adventures.

It was at this point me and John McMillan started running about full time. The change came when he started nipping or courting my cousin Jelly, this put a dent in our friendship causing us to not get along. They obviously wanted me out of the picture. So, it was they two, loved up, and me out in the cold yet again.

I was beginning to get sick of it, going all the way down there in the pissing rain in the dead of winter to find these arseholes rubbering the doors. It was a damn shame in some ways. I had some great times, but there are times in life where you need to grow. Yes, it's hard but can't be avoided.

I became hated by my old crew. Well, hated is a strong word, but definitely not at the top of anyone's Christmas list. Fuck it, that's life. Still, I had no intentions of running about anywhere else or with anyone else. I had grown up with those boys all my life. However, I'm not at liberty to write about the final nail in the coffin, not because there is anything secret or even illegal, the truth is I can only give an opinion. There was no one reason, it was a bunch of different things, one of them being the distance between my home and the scheme I ran about in.

As the end of the first year of the new millennium drew to close, I was writing the last few words in the past decade of my life without even realising it, Carbrain was all I knew. Those streets had given me safety, friendship, hope, love, and fun. Now I was going to turn my back on it with full knowledge of what that would mean.

GRAVITATING TOWARDS THE DARK DAYS (2001)

All the madness of youth was never truer or more evident than in 2001. This was a time where things got totally out of hand. How that year started and ended were two very different sides of the same coin. It began like most others, hungover to the dogs and coming down hard from the chemicals I had ingested the previous night. And if I was unlucky, I was still wrapped around fucking Magilla Gorilla. Believe me, it happened more than once.

Lying in my bed that morning and looking up at the ceiling I realise now my only real problem in life then was waiting for the off-licence too open.

Back in those days, it didn't matter who you were, nobody could buy a drop of booze including Holy Days, Sundays, or Public Holidays even before half twelve in the morning. All that was needed was a wee urge for an early morning tipple.

Spending six hours of a new year's morning in the world of sobriety wasn't even a pin prick on the Richter Scale to me. There I was sixteen years old thinking I had the world by the balls. I had friends, family, and a pretty good life. For me to turn around and say I had any sort of a bad up bringing just wasn't true. I was loved, I was protected as a kid should be and I was even lucky enough to have my stepfather Alex take me, my brother, and my mother away on holidays almost yearly to some amazing places. To be honest nothing happened within my childhood that I can use to blame my bad behaviour.

No, ladies and gentlemen, I take sole responsibility for anything and everything I've done barring that bloody shop getting robbed. Nonetheless, I did have some adults that, instead of putting me straight, taught me some idiotic ideology and because this came from people like my uncles and some of their friends, I sucked that shit up like a sponge; things like how doing time inside some of Scotland's worst Prisons is what makes you a man. Or the other bullshit about how Catholics and Protestants are two very different people, and you don't cross lines. You know stupid shit like that - all the same crap you would get on the streets anyway.

So, I can't and won't put any blame on anyone but myself. It's funny how life can change so drastically in just a few short months. I was nowhere near what you would call trouble-free. All the indictments by now were starting to mount up, one after another after another. Thankfully, at this stage, I was still months away from trial for any of the heavy ones. Still, though, I was going in and out of court like a goddamn revolving door. Small shit, mostly drunken escapades, my mouth getting the rest of my body into hot water. For the most part, the stuff was still small-time, at least the stuff I had been caught for anyway.

Life outside the halls of justice, however, now that was another matter altogether. It seemed like every day I was getting deeper and deeper into the shit. Violence and robbing everything and anyone we could get. You either paid in budda (cash) or blood. It made little difference. I'm not saying this to boast or make light of the day-to-day nasty shit we did. I'm not proud of a lot of stuff we did. I would even go as far as saying I've grown to detest it, but it's important to me that I stay as close to the truth as possible.

THE CRANHILL DAYS

Our first encounter with Stacey Lennox and the whole Cranhill crew came by total accident. Life can be funny that way, you never know what is going to happen and when. Something as simple as taking the wrong bus, can put you on a completely different path. The bus may have taken the correct route that sunny Friday afternoon, but my life was heading for a major detour.

Fact is, we would have had no reason to even be in Glasgow that morning if not for John Duncan and all his drunken antics and with none of us having any reason to take that bus.

Life today would have been very different and not just for me but also for Jay, John, Kelly, Ginger, Stacey Lennox and perhaps even my own family; Stacey Rice our two children Lucas and Madison but none more than for my other son, Paul Jr.

Everything started the previous night with John Duncan what was the date here, or JD as he was sometimes known, out in the street stupidly flashing about a lockback to anyone who was unlucky enough to walk past. Showing off, basically. The best thing about it was that the lockback in question didn't even belong to him. He decided to pinch it from my bedroom when I was in the shower. So, there he was out dancing in the street with the knife in hand like a fucking loony toon. It wasn't even his to begin with, cheeky little swine that he is.

The fact he took it without asking wasn't the issue here. He was forever doing stuff like that. Almost like that annoying older brother who's forever taking your shit without asking, rummaging about your room when you aren't there, more of a pain in the arse than a sneaky thief. Don't get me wrong, anything he took he would always return. He wouldn't dare try and keep it. So, him taking it out, that was no big deal.

Given the number of times he sat in my room messing around with it, I should have just given it to him. Stopped him playing about getting a thrill from the clicking sound it made when he snapped it open. Then again, I doubt that would have made much of a difference. He was obsessed with taking it out and swinging it about the bedroom. That's the knife I'm talking about, not his privates.

All things considered he was still just a teenager like the rest of us so I guess I should give him a pass given his immaturity.

This day though he goes out with the lockback on him, why? I don't know. And within ten minutes, this big Indian policeman that we all called The Turbanator, (a bit of a legend in his own lunchtime,) turned up. Now he was a man who always got his man and, like the nickname suggests, wore a turban. He had come racing up the street along with his wee side kick, a stunning wee blonde bird called Michelle. She was one right sexy wee number to say the least and I'm sure was eventually moved up to the drugs squad.

There was no doubt they had been called by one of my mother's neighbours.

So, Mr Duncan, instead of putting it back into his pocket like a sane person or even walking back into my house - the front door was still open after all, you know, the smart thing to do, John decides the best plan of attack was to launch it right into the fucking street and in full view of the approaching police car a mere few metres away and then he took off running. Leaving Jay and Ginger in pure hysterics as they watched him staggering down the hill looking like a half-drunk rubber band. Which, to be perfectly honest, was no big deal, nothing the of rest of us hadn't or wouldn't have done on a daily basis. We were all by this stage a bunch of degenerates. The only real difference here was it is like twelve in the afternoon and he's already off to see the wizard. That was just John for you, totally off his nut though for the most time in the best possible way.

Even the two polis, whom by then had gotten out of the car and picked up the knife, just stood there in complete amazement at the state of him staggering away. They didn't even bother to give chase. Why would they? After all, they both knew John well and knew that he would pop up again soon enough. At which point they would do him twice as hard, once for the knife and then for whatever else he got arrested for. A dirty wee trick, but one Strathclyde police had become notorious for.

They would sometimes keep charges like these on the back burner for months on end. Then, just as you thought you had slipped through the net, bang! Here comes the inditement. It was a good way of guaranteeing you got remanded if say you had been picked up on some kangaroo charge and they wanted you off the streets. Ninety eight percent of the time charges like shoplifting or a breach of the peace would result in being released on bail on the Monday afternoon but add carrying a knife into that equation and the chances of bail drop to around 20% - and, if you have previous convictions then it was almost guaranteed you'd be sent down.

All the while this is happening outside my door, I'm completely oblivious to any it. I had just come out the shower when I heard my mother's voice from outside the house. She was giving the polis an ear full, for, in her opinion, harassing my mates Jay and Ginger. They were, from what she could see, only standing on her property not bothering anyone coupled with the fact it was happening on her doorstep of all places, well she just wasn't standing for that.

Wee Angie (my mother) is small in height but has the heart of a lion, especially when it comes to protecting her cubs or friends of. All I could hear was her telling these two police officers off and she was going at them.

'These boys are doing fuck all wrong. They're only waiting on my son getting out of the shower... Why don't you's just fuck off and go out and catch some rapist.' (I bet you they've never heard that one before.)

Now these two polis weren't blind or stupid. They quite plainly saw the red handled knife lying in the middle of the road. They also knew John was the culprit not Jay and not Ginger whom, as his nickname implies, had bright orange hair, and stuck out like a one-legged man at an arse kicking party whenever we all stood in a big crowd together.

By now I had come out of the shower, got dressed, and came out the front door. I wanted to know for myself what all the commotion was? Then finally the penny dropped. I saw for myself the knife everyone was talking about!

They had already bagged it up in one of their police evidence bags.

All I could think was: *you're a cheeky sneaky bastard.* If it wasn't bad enough that he had taken it without asking me, he'd only gone and let the polis find it. What a fucking tit!

Meanwhile my mother was still going hard at these two police officers. I mean she's getting out of hand and was coming close to being arrested herself. *Right,* I think to myself, *time to rein her in a bit.*

'Mum calm down before you end up being lifted yourself.' But she was seriously on one, telling them,

'Yous have just taken that knife out your car trying to stitch these boys up. They've done nothing wrong here.'

I could understand her frustration, but she was one hundred percent in the dark on this one. In her mind, they were at the bam up. Police harassment was nothing new to any of us, but we also deserved it. A lot of the time we brought a lot of shit upon ourselves through all the trouble we were causing daily. You can only push the system so far before it pushes back, then you know about it.

Now I was faced with a real dilemma. I couldn't exactly say that's my knife. They would have needed to jail me for my own protection. If my mother thought for one second, I was out in the streets carrying knives she would have killed me on the spot. She had heard stories over the years about me getting into this thing or another but always took my side, that's just the way she was.

Finally, I got her back inside. Then came the usual shite from the polis, checking our names against the PNC system (the police national computer), a national system set up so that if your name pings anywhere in UK they know instantly. So, while they're making sure you have no warrants out for you or that none of their colleagues want to speak with you regarding anything in the past or present, they have you standing like a starfish going through every nook and cranny in the hope of finding anything they can to fuck with your day.

Finally, all our names came back clear, and we were told we were all free to go, but to take a message with us. *Tell John they'd be seeing him soon.*

I wanted to strangle John for what he had done, but that was always John for you. He was never a bad guy, he just done shit sometimes that would get right under your skin. We were probably all guilty of that. I don't think I even got that angry at him for losing it in the first place - what's done is done, just move on. It was more about the inconvenience he caused that pissed me off.

We found John an hour or so later next to Our Lady's High School in the Woodland area. He was already thinking about handing himself into police custody.

'Why?' we all asked in pure bewilderment. His answer was blunt and to the point.

'If I'm caught tomorrow, I'll be detailed all weekend.'

You know something, in a situation like that, his worries were valid. No one wants to be kept in the police cells over the weekend. Ask anyone, from the bottom feeders to all your top end villains. Nobody, not one of them, wants to hear that door slam behind them. The silence is deafening. There are people out there who have done the whole prison experience and would quite happily tell you that given the choice most of them would spend a full week inside prison than spend three days in police custody. You would spend from the Friday to the Monday with nothing, just total isolation, and a cold feeling of loneliness. Still though, for John to hand himself in was nuts, he was definitely looking at prison time, we all knew that.

After an hour or so we talked him down. We decided that the best course of action was to disappear for a few days and take ourselves out the line of fire. It wasn't unheard of for the polis to scoop everyone up for something only one of person was guilty of. They would round everybody up and charge the lot of us with some Mickey Mouse charges, nothing major just something that would keep us all locked up over the weekend. It more of an inconvenience, let's call it the cost of doing business.

So, we were all in agreement the thing to do would be to split up and get the hell out of dodge, even if only for weekend.

'Right. Fuck it lads, I have an idea. Since Johnny-Boy D lost my only lockback I'll be needing a new one. None of us want to be fucking about the streets of Cumbernauld anyway. We'll go to Glasgow tomorrow morning bright and early spend the day fucking about in the city.'

This was around the middle of the summer of 2001. A hot day, though we are talking Scotland not Spain here, so hot is a term I'm using loosely.

Our plan was simple, to stay in Glasgow for as long as possible during the daytime and on returning the following night we'd stay low-key, forget hanging around the usual stops where the polis would almost definitely be on the hunt for John. We'd be smart and keep our group small. Maybe four or five of us at most. This would probably be the hardest part of all as Friday night was party night, and everybody came out. Nothing more attractive to police officers doing the weekend shift than breaking up a mob of drunken teens. So, probably not the best place for a boy on the run to be hiding out in. As for that first night, we decided that if we just stayed in the shadows and off everyone's radar, we would be fine.

I even told Kelly there was no point coming down that night.

When I told her the reasons why she was fine with it. She never asked too many questions anyway. She wasn't one for being suspicious or jealous. If you wanted to have a night out with your mates, *go for it,* that was her way of looking at life. A ploy I unfortunately played heavily upon many times, and I truly regret now.

I don't remember much about that night, certainly nothing exciting happened. I do know John spent the night with our mate Tamlin. She allowed him to stay from time to time - it saved him having to walk all the way back down to Carbrain, or if his mother kicked him out, which by then was every other week. I guess Tamlin just had a good wee heart in her and couldn't see anyone on the streets.

The next day came and for whatever reason Tamlin kicked John out at the crack of dawn. She must have had something on that day or I'm sure she would have let him stay for longer, but the sun was up, and he was out.

Of course, John knew he could bang on my door regardless of the time of day and my mother would let him in. When I say early, it was probably around 10am. He got kicked out of Tamlin's around 7am, God only knows what he did from the time he left Tamlin's to when he chapped my door. I was always up first light anyway so him coming to mine at that time made little difference. Then Jay and Ginger arrived, and finally Bobby turned up.

Now we had a serious problem. The boy Bobby hated John with a passion - usually this wasn't an issue as Bobby never ran about with us. How he even came to be in my room that morning is still a bit of a mystery. The day was already getting off to a bad start. We hadn't even left my home yet let alone Cumbernauld and Bobby is looking like he is ready to take John's head off. You could feel the tension, it was awkward as hell for the rest of us there. None more so though than for me, you see out of everyone there I was John's only real mate, Jay was just starting to take a shine to him. Ginger, I don't think even knew him. And Bobby was wanting to eat him alive. Then in the middle of this shit show here's me trying to cool everything down.

Bobby's attitude towards John was simple-'make sure he stays well clear of me, and I will not slap the shit out of him.'

I think everyone there was more than happy with that situation. I know I definitely was so, with all that shit done and dusted, we all headed out. It wasn't even eleven in morning yet and already the sun was beating down on top of us. We all had money, we all had drink, Jay had his hash. The rest of us hated that shit and now we had a reason to go and mess around in the city all day, but still there was that awkward feeling that it could kick off between those two at any moment. Thankfully nothing ever did. To this day I don't know why Bobby hated John so much, I never asked, it had nothing to do with me. So, who cares. Finally, we got into Glasgow. Buses in those days took close to an hour unlike today, twenty minutes and you are there. We all spent the day messing about Glasgow drinking and carrying on. All of us having fun and letting our hair down.

Then the time came for us to head down to the world famous, well Strathclyde famous, Victor Morris, a shop that was known by neds and outdoor enthusiasts alike. It was a one stop shop that helped to arm almost every ned with any weapon they could afford. And we're not just talking small fold away knifes here either, there were crossbows, machetes, swords, you name it they sold it. Boys in their early teens were walking in and buying knifes big enough to skin a crocodile. And then calm as you like; they would just walk right out the door.

Needless to say, the polis were all over the top of this. For whatever reason seemed powerless to do anything to stop it. Other than if they caught you coming out of the shop underage, they would jail you and without doubt take the offending item off you.

As for shutting the actual shop down though. Who knows how it managed to stay open? As far as we could see they operated with complete impunity. They did have over eighteens only sign on display, so I guess that made everything okay!

By the time we got down there it was close to one in the afternoon. We had been drinking most of the morning too.

Then Jay spotted a man in a suit just standing around outside the shop watching everyone coming and going. Like I said this was the middle of summer and he is rocking the old tin flute. Definitely something wrong with that picture. As soon as Jay pointed him out, we're all in agreement that this guy was, without a shadow of a doubt, CID. I mean, he wasn't even trying to hide it.

'Fuck this lads, we'll come back and get it another day. Forget getting lifted for a poxy lockback. Afterall, we stay in Cumbernauld not downtown Baghdad, I'm sure spending the weekend without a weapon won't be the end of the world.'

Everyone seemed happy with this. No one would have the audacity to just swagger on in there anyway. Well, almost no one. Yip, you guessed it, the one and only Mr Duncan, without a care in the world says,

'Paul, give me the money. I don't give two fucks about the CID.'

I was flabbergasted, I couldn't believe out of all of us standing there he was the only one with enough balls to walk in. Right past the polis. I mean, really! He was the boy they were already looking for and he's doing stuff like that. What can I say? He was totally off his rocker.

To this day I've always suspected that John might have even wanted imprisoned. It happens more than you think. Thankfully nothing like that happened. Though he never got the knife either. For whatever reason he came out with something very large under his arm. Instead of buying the small practical fold away pocketknife he gets a machete or as more commonly known in the Glasgow area, a tenner shot. This is what ten pounds bought you in this shop at the time. I mean, come on John, this is Glasgow not Gaza. 'Why do we need weapons like these?' I asked. He just laughed, shrugging his shoulders and said,

'It's all I could get.'

I give him £30, this cost £10. My powers of deduction told me that the cheeky bastard just pocketed £20 of my money! But that was just John, a loveable rascal.

Now if John thought for a spit second, I would be walking through the city centre with this big jungle chopper up my sleeve he had another thing coming. So, after ten minutes or so of back and forth with him about who's carrying it back home, he gave in. After all he got the blooming thing, so he had little choice in the matter. Finally, we all set off for home with Jay becoming drunker and drunker and starting to get that angry look in his eyes.

'Fuck,' I'm thinking, 'We've been here before and he usually ends up getting into a random fight with someone. This is all we need!'

Thankfully Jay would answer to Bobby and when he told him to 'cut it out,' he complied there and then. We all headed for Buchanan bus station without anything else happening. We got to the bus station just in time to see our bus pulling out of the terminal. By now all I wanted to do was get on the bus, any bloody bus, and head home.

'Let's just get the hell out of this city before we all end up wearing a number on our backs.' I had that gut feeling starting to creep in again and I wanted home.

Thankfully, another bus, the x36, was still there and we all boarded it to take us home. This is what I meant from a spit second decision that can change your whole life forever.

Getting on that second bus instead of the x4 and all the messing about walking up to the bus station even going into the city in the first place everything leads to where I am today for good or bad. It was truly fate.

The x36 bus was one of those long ass journeys that takes you all over the place. One of its stops was Motherson where Stacey and her cousin, my good friend Kathy McGowan, got on.

We had been on the bus for a while. Long enough for us to feel safe about taking the machete from its green sleeve. Me, Jay, and John were messing about carrying on trying to look hard swinging this big fucker about the top deck of the bus.

Ginger was half pissed and I think Bobby had had enough by this stage and was just looking out the window taking nothing to do with the rest of us.

Suddenly Jay started banging the window at whoever was outside.

Two girls getting ready to board.

'Up here, up here.' Jay yelled over and over with an excited tone in his voice. 'Who's that?' I ask getting up from my seat to see who was out there for myself. By the time I got to the window on the other side of the bus the street was empty!

'Who was it?' I asked again.

'Wee Kathy,' he replied.

'Who?' I honesty couldn't think who he meant.

Then the two girls came up top. Honestly my first impression of Stacey wasn't anything special. I don't think I gave her more than two words on that first day. Then I just turned back to speak with Kathy. We both sat there getting a catch up the full way home, two old friends getting a good blether.

Kathy was very interested in why I was sitting with Jay. She was shocked when I told her that I was now running about in Seafar with my Carbrain days behind me. I could tell she was disappointed by the look on her face.

Our stop was coming up with the two of them planning to stay on the bus until the town centre bus stop. Only Jay and John began persuading them to get off the bus at our stop and come down the scheme with us. After a lot of back and forth with Stacey actively encouraging Kathy to come down 'for an hour or so,' fucking longest hour I've ever spent. Lasted almost ten years.

YOUNG ROGUES, YOUNG OFFENDERS

Who could have predicted that the old days were all but gone and the future was looking darker than ever. I for one would never have imagined that by the sweet and tender age of just sixteen years old my life would come to an end.

Okay, I was heading to Prison not the graveyard, but life as I knew it was definitely done. I would soon become a prisoner with years stretching out ahead of me.

Not a name. Not a Person. Just a number

Yet before all that, back in former part of 2001 my incarcerations where still small, nothing to write home about - just a few months at a time. One of the first prison sentences I ever received was for four months. I was caught sitting in the passenger side of a stolen car and sent to Polmont for a short stay.

Others were for daft things like shoplifting or making an ass of myself, drunk, shouting my mouth off with one too many cans of tomato & mozzarella (Stella Artois) in me. That was always a big one for me. I would have one too many shandys and before I knew it, I was a one-man war zone. Well, in my own mind anyway, usually I was just more of a pest than anything.

There were always a few indictments pending on the horizon with some that would have probably resulted in prison time if I hadn't already made up the Court's mind for them with my constant re-offending. At that time, none had come to pass.

So, my drinking adventures weren't always just the shenanigans of a half-pissed moron - sometimes people or their properties were left in ruin.

Still, even though the carnage was almost an everyday occurrence for now my prison time was nothing more than an inconvenience; a very short stay in the juvenile hall of Polmont YOI (Young Offenders Institute). A hall more commonly known as West Wing. This Hall was where all the young ones from the ages of sixteen to eighteen went before being transferred over to halls like North Wing or a few others. The North Wing halls were specifically for young guys from the age of eighteen to twenty-one and from there you're moved up to the cons or adult facilities.

It's funny just how many boys I met back in West Wing as a young sixteen-year-old pup that would go on to be by my side throughout my full prison experience. From short stays in West Wing to being in for the long haul in C Hall within Shotts Prison or in A'B'C and D Hall of Barlinnie Prison, not to mention House Block One in Kilmarnock Prison and even Greenock Prison. No matter the prison, no matter the hall, there was always a 50/50 chance you would bump into one of the guys you started it with all those years ago.

These boys became like your family in a lot of ways!

But before all that. I was nothing more than a ned, running around in a town and city full of them. Just another fuck-up with a knife in his hand that would go on to put me in more than a few sticky situations in Cumbernauld and in Glasgow, well, let's just say if you wanted to pull out a knife in that city you had better use it.

What most people won't know is I only ever used a knife once in Glasgow - the rest of the victims coming from in and around Cumbernauld. All of this happened over the space of three years or so. Not the six weeks that was portrayed in the local and national newspapers at the time.

But before the High Court headlines, the prison time, and even some of the other crimes, there was the Summer of 2001.

At the time Cumbernauld was finished for me. If I was lucky, I was going back there every few weeks at best for quick-change of clothes, pick up some pocket change or money that would fold. Or simply to let my mother know I was still breathing then I would head back into Glasgow. It had become more than just a place to hang out with friends for me, I truly felt accepted by everyone there. You see, compared to where I had grown up, this was like a whole new world where people just walked into each other's homes looking in on one another. There was a real community feeling from each and every one I met. You just didn't get that in my hometown then or even now. During this time, I met a boy whom, without knowing it at the time, would become one of the best boys I ever met.

Unfortunately, he has since passed. His name was Craig Gibb or Gibby as we all knew him. A Riddrie native whose dad was a Barlinnie Prison Officer also known as Gibby. The two of them were we fat dumpy-looking guys who not only shared the same name but looked very similar. One was the other's Mini-me.

Young Gibby was a great guy and a lot of fun to be around, he had a real zest for life with an infectious fun-loving attitude. The two of us became firm friends quickly. He was also the one who stood on the dock beside me for stabbing that rat bastard Gary McCutchen for grassing to my Mum and Stepdad for selling ecto's. Prior to that though we were just to kids in a tower block in Glasgow meeting for the first time.

The night was a Friday, and I was up in the top floor flat in the middle block away up on perhaps the eighteenth of nineteenth level. A bunch of us were all in the kitchen when the ecstasy tablets starting to take hold. That was when Gibby made his entrance.

Nikki was the first to introduce us to one another, nothing exciting just 'Paul this is Gibby! Gibby this is Paul' The two of us could have never known that within the year of that first handshake both of us would be doing relatively large prison sentences. We were forever known to some people as the notorious Gibby and Paul.

Though that night there was nothing out of the ordinarily. Just two young guys having fun, high as fuck, talking shite to one another; the conversation ranging from Yoda to who killed JFK.

Well, when I say having fun this is something I'm using very loosely. Gibby being full of drink and drugs and awed by the view, was constantly getting me to look out the open window of the high-rise block of flats we were in. The view was stunning granted; you could almost see the whole of the Eastend of Glasgow. However, throughout the whole of my life I have been consumed with a crippling fear of heights. So, the more I looked out over the city the worse this fear got. Finally, the sickness and sweats kicked in. I could feel my stomach beginning to go topsy turvy. I tried politely to turn away but Gibby, being drunk as skunk, kept pulling me back towards the window. Finally, the sick came up like a freight train. And whose shoes got it? Not Gibby's, but Charlie's. I mean, of all the people I could have thrown up over it had to be the one girl I was falling hard for.

I told Gibby this story in prison years later and he could hardly stand up with laughter. If one person knew of my big-time crush on her it was him. When he found out the real reason why I boaked he pissed himself for weeks. Of course, any chances I might have had with young Charlie that night were gone due to his persistent pulling me over to that bloody window oh and not forgetting the fact that I gave her shoes my own personal rinse. Gibby rolled almost splitting his sides in hysterics at this. Eventually I couldn't control myself and joined him rolling around the cell floor. This is one of my fondest memories of Gibby and I'm truly sorry he's gone. I guess the only one who probably never found it funny was Charlie though I'm sure she might now.

In terms of my friendship with Gibby, one night together and that was it, we became fast friends. We started phoning each phone and would always meet up in Stacey Lennox's Cranhill flat.

IT'S A SET UP

There were more than a few times over the years Andy pulled me out of both frying pan and fire situations which were always popping up.

Though nothing was more memorable than one very unnerving day in the summertime of 2001. When the Murder Squad had me, Andy and Stacey Lennox all sitting in adjoining rooms connected only by a paper-thin wall within the interview rooms of Easterhouse police office.

Now this was a very dodgy, precarious situation - we truly were in the soup on this one. And, to make matters worse, the circumstances relating to this situation weren't even over. Things were still unfolding right before of us almost in real time. What I mean by this is, while the police were grilling us, they were getting constant updates from the hospital as medics tried desperately to save this man's life.

The polis were setting us up for a fall. In their eyes we were guilty of what would probably become a murder and they had their two main suspects already caught hook, line, and sinker. All they needed to do was to whack us with the ore and have us mounted on the wall of the next policeman's ball.

The stabbing of a boy just outside Stacey's home was bad enough as it was but this one was bad, particularly bad, coupled with the fact it at the time a life was hanging in the balance and could have quite easily turned into a murder at any moment during the interview.

Initially, the polis were only looking to interview us about an attempted murder. However, this was Glasgow; there may have been another three attempted murders across the city that week or there may have been none, but if he died that was going to be a whole new ball game. Innocent or not, any hopes of us being released on police bail would be dramatically cut to virtually zero.

The stabbing in question was that of a boy called Steph Green. This fucking psycho Steph and I had a beef going back a couple of weeks over stupid stuff mostly. It all came to a head and broke out into a fight only an hour or so before he got stabbed. He left after our fight and what happened after that I honestly don't know. Somehow, he managed to get himself stabbed. Given this all happened so close to where we were, it didn't look good.

The polis did what they do best. After hearing about our fight, they did their usual and put two and two together and came up with five. This was far from the first time they've done this to me over the years. This one thing was different, and both Andy and I knew it.

We were innocent. We both knew we hadn't done anything illegal that night. In fact, regardless of the severity, I never left Stacey's house the whole night. And Andy, he was nowhere near the block of flats when it happened. He had met a wee lassie and took her back to her house to make some babies I would imagine. So, you could say he was somewhat busy at the time - it would be very uncharacteristic of him to stop his night of fornicating only to go out and start running around the street stabbing people.

While it may be true that we knew who did this, none of us would ever say a word regardless of how much time has since passed.

The way I see it, this Steph Green was planning on stabbing me that night only he went out and picked a fight with some random people and in the process got almost stabbed to death himself. This is the real nitty gritty of running around the streets with a knife in your hands.

Okay, so here are the facts of what happened that night as best as I can tell you. We were all up the stairs partying away when it happened, and yes me and Steff did have a falling out only an hour or so before the incident took place.

But looking out the window that night we saw him getting into an altercation with a small group of boys. Yet despite being 110% innocent we still got hauled in bright and early the following morning. Evidently the polis, based on their intel, had a very different opinion and were potentially looking to bring down a murder charge on top of our heads!

Walking down the stairs that morning the whole bottom of the close was just red with blood, on the ground, the walls, the steps. I mean it was everywhere. That coupled with the fact the entrances front and back were all taped off. Inside the quarantine zone was just full of police in uniform, CID and most importantly, men and woman in white suits. Out the back of the flats in the bin area they were even on their hands and knees going through everything, pulling out all the bins, sifting through every blade of grass. It was the full nine yards.

Seeing all that, honestly, I thought he was already dead.

If there was one good thing, we could take from this whole fiasco it's this; when you're getting your balls dragged across the flames over things such as this you tend to see a person's true character, not to mention your own.

When you're all alone in a wee grey box room with no friends, no family, no nothing but two members of the CID unit looking to bang you up forever, it can be quite a hard thing to explain to anyone who has never experienced it. You have to have sat there inside those rooms with police officers who are experts at getting inside your head and turning your own words against you to fully understand. Chances are you'll probably never truly get the severity of it.

I've seen and heard of guys, and I mean real bad ass motherfuckers, who have cracked under the pressure of the Polis getting inside their ear and fucking with them.

These days being a police informant is more common than ever – and why not? A guy turns rat because now there are no consequences – it seems like no one cares about the old codes now.

Growing up as a boy you would hear stories from the old boys who were still living that life of how being a grass in their day was considered a death sentence, but I doubt that was wholly true.

On the other hand,, when the polis put the pressure on, you get to know who to trust. When, after a six-hour roasting in a small wee sweat box, the people who are real will usually take it on the chin regardless of the charge in question and never open their mouths. Whereas other guys you thought where solid turn out to be pure marshmallows and start cliping on everyone just to avoid doing a single night in prison.

Andy Lennox was made of pure iron with the heart of a lion. I knew there was never anything to worry about that day. Having people like that next to you make all the difference.

Through this experience Andy learned that I could be relied upon, Even though the Polis had the wrong people in front of them it didn't necessarily mean they would go any easier on you, We both got to know the strength of one another and if we were ever to be arrested on something we were truly guilty of we would know where we stood.

Undoubtably, both of us had the opportunity to size one another up that day but if anything was to make us snap it was the intense heat. Getting locked up at the best of times is murder but when they grabbed us it just happened to be the hottest day in the history of Easterhouse. All day we had to sit there feeling the heat from the polis and melting from the sun beating through the windows behind us. It was horrific.

Six hours later after fingerprints and photos were taken we were then told we were to be released on police bail but with the caveat that we were definitely people of interest and could be picked up again at a later stage.

Honestly, I was just happy to be getting out of that hell hole, though it wouldn't be the last time I was to see the inside of their cells. Thankfully not for anything near as serious.

Fortunately, Steph Green woke up and it just all went away so who knows what ever happened with that one? I guess I never will. Though years later I heard from him of all people that all the blame was put on me. Thankfully he believed me, and it finally got put to bed.

Unfortunately, the fact that Andy and I both got our balls kicked for hours on end did nothing to bring us any closer in the longer term. We just never quite got along with each other. Not that he ever came right out and said it. You could sometimes feel the tension between us when we were both drunk - there would be dirty looks but that's about it. With that said though, he would always have had my back that much was certain.

Stacey also had another brother, Joseph and almost from the get-go we became like brothers.

Growing up back home everyone heard stories about the Lennox brother's cousin - a complete head banger from

Glasgow that would come through from time to time and run about the streets, mad as a hatter, along with his cousin Ian.

Ian was the oldest brother of the Lennox boys, Neil, Graham, and Brian. There were also two sisters, but they are of no consequence to this story.

Now Ian was in my opinion the scariest guy alive. He always scared the shit out of me growing up. I would do my best to stay on his good side. Then again, anytime we ever talked with one another he came across as very polite and respectful and, to be honest, a decent guy.

Going back to (Joseph) Josie as he was better known, before the time we became like brothers there was a situation that caused a big rift between Josie and John Duncan. I had no part in it– but effectively my loyalties were torn.

This left me in a sticky position. I knew that the more I was to run around in Cranhill with Stacey and the rest of that crew I would inevitably bump into Josie. Then I would have to make a decision; be polite and explain to him that he seems like a nice guy but for me to stand there talking away to him behind John's back would make me a bit of a scumbag! Or do I say fuck it, this has got nothing to with me? Thankfully at that stage in 2001 he was still inside serving a seven-year stretch for robbing a post office that you could say, never quite went to plan. He had already served around four years at that point so it was highly likely our paths would cross sooner or later! This constantly played on my mind, I would think about it day and night. Realistically I shouldn't have because John would frequently come through and party with us...

So, was there even a problem?

What would I even do if I saw Josie anyway? Okay, I might have some balls, but if the rumours about him were to be true this guy was a fucking lunatic!

Besides, what, if anything, would John ever do for me? If the tables were turned would John go down swinging all in the name of standing strong for his mate? Probably not. So, I decided even before I first ever met Josie that it would be best just to stay clear of the whole situation.

And then one afternoon a few months later we all appeared in Bellrock Street. There were a few marked police cars sitting outside the block of flats we were heading to but this was nothing new. They would park there from time to time, get out, do a walk around the street then get back in and drive on.

Also parked there that summer afternoon were a few unmarked cars. This usually set off alarm bells in our minds. Generally, seeing a bunch of unmarked police cars usually meant they were there to do a drugs bust of some kind.

Even this ominous sight didn't put us off and we continued to head up over the small patch of grass and into the block of flats itself.

Now, there wasn't anything any of us had to avoid them for. Well, nothing on that day anyway! Still though, you'd think our antennas would be up irrespective of guilt or innocence. However, at that stage on a Friday afternoon all we had on our minds is the upcoming weekend and all the shenanigans to be had. So, the three of us. Me, Jay, and Martin Graham all continued up the staircase.

The objective was to get Stacey and Nikki to accompany all of us along to Blackhill, a scheme just a few miles away from where we were. The plan was simple, all five of us would all take a walk over to Martin's house and hit his mum and dad for a sub - a small loan, not a sandwich, in the hope they would give him enough to cover his weekend. I had my wages already in the bank, so I was all good. Jay had some money of his own. That just left Martin dragging his feet. Worse-case scenario, I would have no doubt subbed him some shillings if it came to it but I could have done without it.

As the three of us covered the short distance between the phone box and Stacey's block of flats we saw this big, bald, lump of a man.

He was standing on the second balcony watching us like a hawk. In hindsight one of us, or possibly all of us, should have thought to ourselves there's something very dodgy going on here. We didn't have any reason to think this way, there was no warrants, unpaid fines, or charges.

The worst thing we had to worry about - was the bags of Jack and Jills in both mine and Jay's pockets. There weren't even that many, just enough to cover the weekend. That was it.

Walking up the block that afternoon there was still nothing that seemed out of the ordinary until the three of us reached the middle landing.

Suddenly I was grabbed, not that it was me they were there for that day, I just happened to be the first of the three of us to make it to the top step.

There was this big lump again, only this time he was ragging me about the landing like an empty tracksuit. He asked me in a rapid-fire manner, 'Where is Josie Lennox?

It took me a few seconds for his question to even sink in. By this point he had me almost coming off my feet. Still holding on to me he homed in, wanting to know my name? By then other officers were coming out of Stacey's home where, as it turned out, a whole bunch of them were conducting a search in the hope of finding Josie.

At which point, I'm half grinning showing off to my mates saying, 'If you want to know where he is just ask her Majesty. I know she's letting him stay with her in one of her many fine establishments. Try Shotts, Kilmarnock or if he is lucky maybe even Corntonvale. I'm sure you will come across him in one of them.'

My two mates stood there laughing away to themselves, but this only served to make him more angry and aggressive.

'You think you're funny ya wee wanker!' came the reply. Okay, of course I was trying to be a funny boy. I was oblivious to the fact that Josie had been moved to an open prison, let alone having gone and absconded from it.

So, when this big ape began drilling me in the middle of the street for information as to his were abouts I was totally in the dark. Not that I would have ever said anything anyway but still.

Now came the worrying part, my immature response had brought them to the decision to do a PNC.

As I have already stated, we knew we had nothing to worry about. All it would take is one simple search of our tracksuit pockets and me and Jay would have been heading for a weekend in the cells.

Fuck me I thought, *why did I have to open my big mouth*? But that was me -always the smart arse. Then came a crackling voice over the police radio the best response I could have hoped for – *there is nothing'* and at virtually the exact same time as the voice on the radio stopped talking, out walked the rest of the police search team.

'Come on guys! He's not here,' said a voice standing near to the back of the group. Then the polis all exited walking down the stairs and back into their cars - none of them looked particularly annoyed. To them it was just another day at the office. They knew they would catch him at some point.

No sooner were they were out of ear shot, and barely containing the excitement in my voice I asked Stacey, 'What the fuck was all that about?

All she could say was they were on the hunt for her brother and that she couldn't tell anyone outside of the family.

Andy and a few others told us what was happening. This made me and Jay think we should start to show off somewhat, stand there and try to associate ourselves with the situation that was unfolding.

Like I've said, we were young and stupid at the time. Given the fact that this big copper gave us a bit of a hard time, to us it provided the platform to start bragging that we had pockets full of pills. We figured if the mob (Scottish slang for police) had half a brain, we would have been heading for Baird Street police station.

Now we knew these guys were there for an absconded prisoner and couldn't give two fucks about some cheeky wee bastards with a few pills on them. Still, it did feel good to stand there playing the part.

Long after they had left and it all calmed down, I pulled Stacey aside and again asked her, 'Why did you not tell me about your brother and the fact he was on the run!' Again, she came back with the same reply. It was so fucking comical I had to just walk away shaking my head.

'We must keep it totally within the family!'

I almost fell over laughing but just had to turn away and leave the conversation. Here I was sitting there with the reincarnation Don Carlo Gambino.

After that we both went back into the flat and started to get ready for the weekend. Around nine pm, as we all partied in her room, Stacey pulled me out into the hallway to talk away from the blasting rave music that boomed from the big black hifi system in her room.

'My brother Joseph wants to meet you, Paul.' And there it was. The moment! I had been dreading. I remember the apprehension mixed with eagerness and excitement. There had been so many stories over the years that it was going to be good to put a face to the name. And so, the two of us slipped out the flat and off down Bellrock Street to a group of three tower blocks situated just across from the local shop.

'Is this where he's been hiding the whole time?' I asked. It wasn't the best of spots. There was always a heavy police presence there at the best of times mostly due to it being a drug dealing hotspot.

'No,' she replied. 'He is up the top of this first tower block.'

Great I thought, we have to go back up to the top of these high flats yet again. What is it with these people can't they keep their feet on the ground for more than a day?

The closer we got to the main entrance the more my phobia of heights began to kick in. I was already sweating like Michael Jackson during his last trial from the ecstasy I'd taken. Now, mix in the thought of being nineteen floors above sea level and my wee bum was making buttons.

Against my better judgement I followed her into the tower block and up to the top floor. Stacey opened the front door and we both walked down the long hallway. Everything was in darkness. Either they were loving the fact this whole thing was scaring the shit out of me or the fucking hobo couldn't afford a light bulb. No matter the reason, all I wanted to do was get back down to earth. I just wanted out of this. This was it the moment of truth, finally I was going to meet this guy.

What a fucking let down! Honestly, I didn't know what I thought he was going to be like but as I walked in, there was this wee guy sitting across the other side of the room who looked about fourteen, his feet barely touched the floor. I thought *is this a wind up.* Then the unthinkable happened. He stood in front of me, and I found myself looking down on his balding head thinking, *this can't be the BIG Josie Lennox surely? This wee guy would get asked for identification to buy fags.*

I'm also thinking, *how can this fucking juvenile-looking wee guy have a such a reputation as one real dangerous badass motherfucker?* But height, strength and body mass have nothing to do with it. When it all comes down to it it's what's in your heart that counts.

I found his actions very misleading. I was expecting some muscle-bound potty-mouth for lack of a better description and what I got was a very well-spoken guy. It took the wind out my sails and knocked me back a bit.

Our first encounter with one another was very pleasant, I have to say. For the best part of that night we took some sweets together, always a great way to break the ice and talked away making jokes and even talking about the future. We were having such a good time two subjects never came up: one, my crippling fear of heights and two, his almost imminent return to custody.

After a few hours we decided to walk back over to Stacey's. A stupid move on his part. He walked over with us right into a well-lit Bellrock Street, right past three or more street cameras and up the staircase to her home. I remember thinking all the way over, *this guy is fucking nuts. He must not give two fucks about getting arrested.*

To my amazement nothing happened. No police came near the door not even for a noise complaint, not that it ever happened through there anyway but still, talk about thumbing your nose to the government. This guy had no fear.

As the night rolled to a close, he pulled me into the kitchen and said, 'It's been a real pleasure to meet you Paul and we will definitely be keeping in touch,' and then he left.

It was to be another five years before I was to see him again. He was caught two days later and returned straight to Barlinnie prison. Six months later I was to follow him. As he was coming to the end of his incarceration mine was just at its beginning. Of course, we did not know this at the time, although looking back on it all, there could be no other place for us.

Life was becoming darker by the day. The violence, the drinking, the drug taking - it was all getting out of hand and everyone could see it. My mother by this stage was scared for me every time I left the house. Anticipating the night I wouldn't return and instead of the police chapping her door to tell her I was yet again in custody, they would be there to tell her that I had been found dead in some doorway somewhere. Making my mother live through that is something that now as an adult with kids of my own will be something that I will always carry with me.

'WATCH YOUR COMPANY KID'

By now my phone was full of everyone's numbers who all went around to Stacey's house. We all started to jump around with one another daily and not just when Stacey was there either. Sometimes I came through and went straight round to other associates like the Tortolano brothers Paul and Mark, and if not them, wee John McFarland, and his brother Kevin. Then there was Wee Wiggy who was always coming up from Parkhead along with a few more. Not to mention of course, Nikki, whom I was with almost every day back then.

There were also a lot of other girls; Stacey's cousins, Angela Lindsay. and her oldest sister Elaine and her man John. I must mention one girl who put it on a plate for me, but to bang her meant going over the bridge into Rauhazie, somewhere I had been told not to ever go unaccompanied under any circumstances. There they would see me as an enemy and to them dealing out violence at the drop of a hat was no big thing.

This warning came from everyone in Cranhill, and one I took to heart. This was a pity as wee Pudding, as she was known, would have gotten her wee kebab well and truly battered. Then again, was her wee Gucci Pucci worth getting a kicking or worse for if any of that young team on that side of the bridge happened to stop me? Probably not! So that was just one of those things I just had to let go. We became somewhat friendly in the longer-term, God only knows what ever happened to her.

2001 was a great year for all of us and for the most part we never stepped on anyone's toes - a hard thing to do back then. There was always some sort of danger to navigate albeit quite subtle.

Then there were situations you just knew to stay away from, things like building sites. You might think, what do bricks and mortar have to do with dangerous situations? Well, the buildings themselves had nothing to do with hardcore criminals but believe me, the security firms were all fronts for some serious organised crime groups. Everyone knew this and almost all of us understood that messing around with these places was a good way to find yourself underneath one of those unfinished homes. Everyone that is, but Jay. Then came the one fateful night that heralded the beginning of putting the final nail in the coffin between our friendship.

It all started with Jay and a few boys from both Cranhill and Blackhill they all stayed out in Bellrock Street, drunk as skunks doing what daft young boys do. I had stayed behind with Stacey as she was finally going to lie-down on the bed and allow me entry into her holy temple if you get my drift. So, the choice was to either go out with the boys in the cold figuratively speaking or stay in.

Anyway, God only knows where they spent that night, to this day I still don't know but the following morning in walked Jay, Martin Graham, Brian Taylor, and a few others all looking dead eyed from yet another hard night on the razzle. Nothing new there and as far as I was led to believe, nothing to report.

How wrong I was!

It turned out these fucking maniacs were running around the building site at night playing on the scaffolding, going in and out the houses doing daft stuff - no harm done there. Things changed when the security guard came out his wee hut and Jay launched a fire extinguisher at him from the top of the scaffolding almost hitting the poor guy. Now that *was* a problem. This security guy had been told *don't phone the police, phone these heavies*. Not that anyone of the boys knew this. They were just running mad around the site that night but didn't realise the fact that no police ever came only meant one thing. The guy went back into his hut shut the door and, according to them, that was that it was all over and done with.

Later that day both me and Jay returned home to Cumbernauld unaware of the shite storm that was heading our way, especially me. Jay's name had been given as Jamie Carrol not Jay McCarrol - but my name they knew all too well. In fact they had every little detail about me, which was the biggest fucking joke I ever heard as I wasn't even there. They had my name within two days, everything from who I was to where I came from. I've always known deep down that the information given came from someone within our wee group and I think I know who, but without ever getting proof I'll just let it be.

After a few days I returned, only to find out some serious people were looking for me. I asked why and who? Then the penny dropped, and it all came out. I was beyond raging; my blood was boiling. Of course, Jay. He was standing there without a care in the world. Who cares was his attitude but deep down you could see the concern in his eyes and rightly so. This was how some of these guys put their hard-earned drug money to good use.

And here comes two wee fannies starting to fuck everything up intentionally or not - they were out for blood, and they weren't listening to reason. This was a bad position to be in. There was a lot of fear, no question. We could run and hide. It had worked before, but I also had my uncle Vinnie's voice in my head telling me over and over don't ever run from your troubles, it usually only makes matters worse.

On the other hand, these where some scary, frightening looking S.O.B's so taking off for a while might not have been the worst idea. Stupidly, we thought sticking around was probably the best move but after a day or so Jay got itchy feet and headed back to Cumbernauld. I was still in Cranhill when four black Range Rovers rolled up looking like something out of an old Gangster flick. Then out stepped several mean looking bastards, all falling in line behind this big lump with a scowl on his face, the sort of scowl that would bring grown men to their knees and then there was me, this wee piss-ant-nobody standing there trying not to look scared.

He stood there and shouted, 'Paul, get down here ya wee prick.'

What could I do? Fuck it! I swallowed my fear and headed down to the four cars with their engines still idling and the group of heavies awaiting me. My heart was pumping, my adrenaline spiked and sweat ran down the back of my neck as I headed down each flight of stairs towards what could have been my last day on earth.

When I got to the bottom of the outside staircase there stood before me a bunch of muscle-bound scar-faced men all looking like they were ready to pounce at a moment's notice. My stomach was like a washing machine churning with the crippling fear of the unknown. All I wanted to do was take off, but I also knew that that wouldn't help, I would be always on alert, always looking over my shoulder. And for what? Something I had nothing to do with. No, the best thing I could do was just play it out and hope for the best.

As I got within grabbing distance to them one came towards me.

He was a small but equally scary looking guy, he grabbed me by the scruff of the neck and frog marched me into the back of a waiting Range Rover. Then bang, within the blink of an eye we were speeding down towards the same building site where it all happened a few nights previously. I was dragged before the security guard that Jay had almost hit with the red extinguisher.

As good as it was to see the one guy who could prove my innocence, I was still in the middle of a fucking building site and on a Sunday afternoon of all things. The whole place was totally deserted; the perfect place to slap the shit out me or, if I was unlucky, I'd end up buried in the concrete helping to hold up somebody's new home.

To my immense relief the guard had a good eye for memory and straight away told them, 'He had nothing to do with it.'

My heart was in my mouth but then I knew categorically that facing them was by far the best move. Suddenly the whole mood changed; everyone was talking *to* me instead of *at* me. Although they were far from satisfied, they still wanted to know who this Jamie Carroll was. Obviously, I knew exactly who they meant, but to rat. now that is somewhere I just couldn't go so I played like a Dum Dum until I could see they were starting to get pissed off with me. In the end I just came clean.

'Yes, I know him.'

But me standing there and becoming a rat! I've never grassed on anyone, especially not Jay. The boy was like my brother, I just could not bring myself to go there. I think in the end they may have even respected me for it. After about ten minutes or so they told me to fuck off and walk back. Then a bald gravel-voiced man barked,

'Wait.' When I turned around, he had already opened the back door of one of the cars he was standing beside. My heart sank, was this it? Had they changed their minds and decided that my life wasn't worth the paper it was printed on?

I'm glad to say he was merely being a gentleman and ran me back to HQ. On the short run back, he gave me something to think about,

'Watch your company, kid!'

The second I was out the car everyone there was saying how they were just about to get teamed up and march down to face them. Bullshit! Sometimes it's just easier to say nothing and move on.

This was probably the most terrifying situation I've ever experienced and believe me I've had a few hairy moments in my time. I had never been so glad to see the back of them.

After that episode, Jay and I gradually became more and more distant, I think both of us were somewhat saddened by this. I know I was. After that night we would never be as close again.

It's not fair on Jay for me to sit here and put sole responsibility on him. For me to say that the break down in our friendship was entirely his fault well, it's just not accurate, I put more than my fair share into fucking it all up. The building site situation was, if nothing else, just the straw that broke the camel's back.

Jay was still coming through most days, we even went in and out of Glasgow together sometimes, though no sooner we got there then we would both go our separate ways and stand in different groups. Actions speak louder than words.

Even on the nights we were at house parties together people could see and even feel the divide between us. It was strange, here were two guys that, from the outside, looked as though they were ready to kill one another, yet at the first sign of trouble we were right back together side by side ready to fight the world.

UNPREDICTABLE LIFE IN THE SCHEMES

The uncertainty of scheme life meant that you had to be on your guard, there were codes and expectations that had to be followed and stepped up to. A prime example of his happened one night when I got into a beef with a boy from Blackhill. It was all over a bottle of Buckfast and a derisory comment about Cumbernauld.

The moment the boy and me stepped onto the grass for a fight, Jay hit some random boy with a brick. The worst thing about that was this poor guy came from Easterhouse I think and had nothing to do with any of it. The two of them started boxing with one another rolling about on the grass where, by now, me and this boy are punching lumps out of each other. From there, the boy I was fighting with had a friend who tried to get involved, only for Neil, my boyhood friend from Cumbernauld, to lamp him.

One silly comment turned into a dress rehearsal for World War three and we were all knocking the fuck out of each other. Thankfully the fights never lasted long and afterwards we all had a good laugh about it.

Life in schemes like this could be unpredictable, with violence always being just on the horizon. Of course, it wasn't always just fisticuffs and handbags at dawn. At the drop of a coin, it could become extremely violent and nasty. Like the night wee John McFarland stabbed a boy almost to death outside the phone box in Bellrock Street for nothing more than asking for fifty pence off him to use the phone. To John, it was just another junkie asking for money. His reaction was excessive to say the least. Like any normal person he could have just politely told him to fuck off but instead he pulled out his lockback knife and stabbed him to within an inch of his life.

The first any of us even knew about this was when his then girlfriend Stacey Macpherson came running up to the second-floor flat shouting for help to get John off this poor unfortunate fellow. Though by this point it made little difference, John had already stopped his frenzied attack and was just watching him on his hands and knees with blood pissing from him.

As we all shouted at him to get off the streets, he just stood there like he was in a daze. Thinking back now, it's probably safe to say he was in complete shock at what he had just done.

Within minutes of us all gathering on the outside balcony the Polis had arrived, arrested John on the spot, and called an ambulance for the guy who by now was on death's door. That boy survived, but others in similar situations on the scheme wouldn't. John was remanded to a children's home and charged with attempted murder. That would be the last I would see of wee John until doing time with him in Polmont a few years later - he was still doing the same sentence for the stabbing.

We had been running about this scheme for less than four months now and already there had been two stabbings and a slashing outside the shop - what that was about God only knows - gang fights occurred almost nightly. The scheme was out of control and so we fitted in well.

It was around this time stories from various sources were increasingly coming back to me that the guy I was doing illegal activities with was, for some mad reason, bad-mouthing me to anyone with a pair of ears. He was telling everybody out there that I was nothing more than a money-making puppet dancing on his string. Why did he do this? Who the fuck knows!

It's something I never did get to the bottom of. I mean I was bringing this cocksucker an envelope full of cash on a weekly basis and he was telling everyone with a pulse that I was the biggest Bam this side of the Mississippi. Still, talk is cheap and some of the people that were telling me this had their own agendas. So, I wasn't ready to condemn him just at that time.

However, those stories were coming from somewhere and needed investigated. I decided to err on the side of caution and bide my time and so I put it to the back of my mind and kept an ear to the ground.

A SIGNIFICANT MEETING

Again, it was a weekend. Stacey Lennox's house was full but, unlike most Fridays, we were all allowed in into the living room where her mum spent most of her day. The only time you even heard that woman's voice was to get one of us to walk down to the off sales for her. Apart from that, you forgot she was even there.

Stacey's room was down at the bottom of long hallway next to the front door so when you walked in there was no real reason to walk down to living room. Not on this night though, for whatever the reason Carol was getting her groove on along with us. I was sitting on an armchair with Janice on my knee while I talked with Lindsay Lennox, Stacey's cousin and the first Glaswegian Lennox, I ever met in all the places was Cumbernauld High School. She had been shipped through our way to stay out of trouble. It never played out that way and before we knew it she had been shipped home.

Lindsay is a great girl. When I first met her back in 1998 she was sitting on the wall outside Milcroft shop wearing more gold than King Midas. It's safe to say I liked her immediately.

As we sat chatting away there was a guy a good few years older than me talking in the corner with Stacey. It was obvious he was chatting her up, but what did I care? For one I was still with Kelly at the time. Two, I was banging her behind big Harry's back and three I had my eye on her pal. So basically, I was like, 'You're not my bird, what the fuck do I care what you do?' Only now he's talking to her loudly enough that the full room hears him telling her 'Come down to my house. Let me get a ride at you, who cares what that wee prick from Cumbernauld says I will burst him anyway.' Then with his full hand he grabbed her by the old female tunnel of love and lifted her up an inch or two. Then he smiles right at me.

Cheeky bastard I thought then I turned and saw the full room looking at me in pure shock. Like I said, under any other circumstances I wouldn't have blinked an eye but there was this cheeky little monkey almost shouting from the rooftops, 'Come ahead Paul.' What could I do? I had to retaliate.

I shouted across the living room, 'Here prick, you got a fucking problem with me? Let's sort it out here and now.' That's all the push he needed. He started acting like a fucking lunatic, screaming down the house.

All the noise must have alerted Andy, whom I later refer to as Cotton Candy, Stacey's older brother. He was a small, skinny, almost crippled looking wee guy. He looked like a strong wind would send him flying down Bellrock Street. Anyway he burst through the living room door, his face puce with rage, shouting at both of us, 'Who the fuck do yous think yous are starting a fucking fight with my mother sitting here?' Then my friend and saviour Nikki grabbed Cotton Candy by the arm and took him into the hall. The two of them had become a bit of an item prior to this stage so she was probably the only one that could have calmed him down. Whatever was said out there I don't know but he returned a different man. Just five minutes earlier he was growling at me, now suddenly he was winking at me. What the fuck got said? Who knows? But his attitude had totally changed.

He began the conversation with, 'Listen boys, don't be daft here. The two of you are just steamed up, no point fighting over something so trivial. Come on Steph I will walk you out.'

What happened next, I can only talk about with limited details as the only two real names I can use are my own and Andy's who has since unfortunately died and is beyond the reach of prosecution. As for the others involved let's just called one of them Biscuit and one Soup.

So basically, Andy told Steph Green to go and wait outside and that he would be down in two minutes. Then he pulled me into the kitchen. The first words to come out his mouth were, 'Paul, I've just saved your life there, kid.'

Now at the time, I'm young full of piss and fire and wanting to defend my name. I wasn't taking the time to stop and think about this guy; who he is, what he's capable of, stuff like that. All I wanted to do was look tough, show people I was willing to go the extra mile if need be. Andy, he knew him all too well and more importantly just what he was capable of. So, after a to-the-point talking to from Andy, I stayed up the stairs while Andy went down to sort it out. That was it. There was no mention of fighting and none of stabbing him, but the street can turn on you that quickly. I'm not party to whatever was said between them, but after he insulted a female very close to Andy's heart it all turned turbo. Andy stabbed him a few times then Soup stabbed him after that, ending up with both running to a safe house to change and get off the streets. I happened to witness it all unfold from the window.

A few minutes later in walked Biscuit, a very dangerous and unpredictable boy who I was close with at the time. He summoned us, 'Guys, guys, guys. Come quick, come quick.' He stood there like the cat that got the cream with one big ass cheesy grin on his face.

Now of course I knew what he was talking about but no one else did. So down we went to the bottom of the staircase where Steph was lying. He was very still, zero movement coming from him. I thought he was already dead and with Bellrock Street being a hot spot for police at the best of times all I wanted to do was get the fuck out there.

It never played out like that. Biscuit decided that if he wasn't dead he soon would be and stabbed him a dozen more times. It was a sickening sight, the guy may have been an arse but he was defenceless, and likely already dead. I remember thinking to myself, *enough is enough I'm not doing life for this shit*. I think Nikki and Big Harry had the same idea because the four of us spit up right there and then Nikki and Harry went back home to Riddrie. I went back up the stairs and Biscuit went where he went.

Meeting Andy, Stacey's brother proved to be a catalyst. For a start he inducted me into the street school of economics. Unfortunately Andy has now passed so I feel at liberty to talk about some of the events that were to make an indelible mark on my life and lead me into other significant events. Andy showed me that my set up for selling the pills was all wrong. Now, Andy missed his calling in life; it's always a shame to see anyone squander their talent away. In his case, he was smart as a whip with a real head for numbers and could tell me how much more money I would have in my pocket each week if I was to stop all this silly spending on booze, buying trainers and, my favourite past time, having all-night party's where the ecto's were on us. That was how reckless myself and Jay had become. If it wasn't me doing it in Glasgow it was Jay doing it in Cumbernauld.

Now, with the all-night party's even a Dum Dum knew that that was a daft thing to do. So, after that all stopped and I calmed down buying new trainers every other day, (something Andy got me into in the beginning I might add,) more money started to stack up in my pocket.

Then he taught me about other drugs and how much more money he was making doing them. Now I can sit here today and write about this as he has been dead now a while, but if he was still out in the street, I would never write about anything that could potentially get him or anyone else for that matter, indicted.

You know, a lot of the times we never saw eye to eye, but I will say this, I respected and admired the hell out that man and was sad when I heard of his passing. He was a small, skinny wee guy with about four hairs on his head or perhaps his blonde hair just made it look that way. When it came to a fight well, I'd seen him in action and fuck me could he shift. He was also very loyal and charismatic fellow, all things you look for in a person.

MORNING AFTER THE NIGHT BEFORE

I was awoken by the sound of a dog barking in the distance and the brightness of the sun splitting through the window. I stumbled into the kitchen half asleep looking for a drink, my mouth dry from a yet another night of heavy drinking.

My attention was drawn to something happening outside on Bellrock Street. From the small kitchen window, I was horrified to see the full block of flats was taped off with police tape. My heart sank. All around were Police officers in white suits on their hands and knees lining the street, going over the road with a fine-tooth comb.

Right there and then I felt sure that the boy Steph had died. I could virtually feel the colour drain from my face to white. I ran back into the bedroom and woke Stacey. 'Get up you. Get out of bed now. The bloody Murder Squad are everywhere.'

Finally she got her lazy ass out of bed and we both crept over to her bedroom window trying our hardest not to be seen or make a sound. Sure enough police were out the back as well. They were going through every bin, every bush, every blade of grass. All you could see was a sea of white forensic suits. At the same time all this was being monitored by a woman in a Tyvek forensic suit taking photos of every move they made.

'Fuck me,' I thought, 'this is serious.'

Of course, Stacey was standing there playing the John Gotti card trying to downplay it and make out like it was just another Saturday morning; like this shit happens every day – no big thing. That was her way, a ned who glorified violence, always talking tougher than she was. That day she was saying things like, 'So what the fuck if he is dead. He was a prick anyway.'

I remember just looking at her thinking, 'Don't talk shite ya fucking bullshitter, no one is that cool especially when it comes to a murder.'

She knew it had nothing to do with her and that's why she was playing the big yin. Still by that point even I was thinking to myself, *this has fuck all to do with me either.*

I hadn't been standing at the window long when the inevitable happened. One of the men in white looked right at us, I mean, he literally pointed up at the window then turned to his mate and said something in his ear. I don't think ten seconds passed before the door was getting hammered off its hinges.

There wasn't much point in ignoring the door. They'd already seen us. Stacey let them in and to my surprise, along with six or seven what looked like CID, was her brother Andy. Handcuffed.

What the fuck's going on here?' I'm thinking. Why is Andy already in cuffs? I mean, what are they going to do? Detain us here and put us in different bedrooms while they try and take statements?

My bewilderment was soon answered when they told him to show them the clothing he had on the night before. He passed them a crumpled-up tracksuit and jumper that were then placed in a brown paper evidence bag.

Then their attention turned to Stacey. I heard them tell her that she was being detained under Section 16 due to a very serious incident that happened the night before.

Being detained under Section 16 in Scotland means that you can be held without charge for up to six hours. Usually this only happens when you are under indictment.

I was next. The CID officer turned to me and looked at me steadily. Up until that point, I had been trying my hardest to blend into the background and not be noticed.

'What's your name son?'

The moment I heard the words coming from his mouth, I knew I was in for one hell of a day. Just how bad would soon become apparent.

Both of us were handcuffed and told to show them any clothes we had on from the previous night. Not hard for me, I was already fully dressed.

I had been planning on getting out the city for a few days, let the heat die down. Even though I had nothing to do with it, I knew kicking about around the ones who did was just bad karma.

At this point a big mean looking copper turned away from us all and started talking into his daft big radio. In those days police radios looked more like a black brick than a communication device. The copper was telling whoever was on the other end to cancel checking out the address in Cumbernauld because at this end they had detailed an I.C. one male, the one they were looking for.

Alarm bells began seriously ringing in my head. How do they have my parents' home address? Why am I getting pulled into this pish? How do they even know me? Who have they been talking too? A million thoughts ran through my mind.

Right Paul, let's stop and think here, chances are they know about the little bit of a ding dong I had with him last night, that's all it could be.

I had no doubt in my mind, we would go back to the station and the rest of the troops would be there, all lined up waiting to get taken into interview rooms. All the polis were doing was fishing, trying to put the pieces together.

As soon as we got to the bottom of Stacey's block of flats and I saw all the blood, I knew it was over. I felt sick to my stomach. If he was dead, this could be the final nail in my coffin. Not only was the guy murdered he was fucking butchered. The state of the close on its own was enough to testify to that.

The best way I could describe it – it was as though one very large slug left one big ass blood stain. Like when a slug leaves a horrible gooey mark on the ground, only in this case it been left by that poor bastard crawling very slowly across the walkway from the back of the close to the front before being found by Jamba, who had been returning home from a night out.

Jamba immediately called an ambulance. That was only thing that saved the guy's life, though at this point none of us knew that. I remember thinking, having seen all that blood, *how the hell did he manage to call for help?*.

The drive to Easterhouse Police station was quick and before we knew it the three of us were all in different rooms getting the grilling of a lifetime. We all knew the rules: 'No comment,' to every question, it was our only lifeline. The more questions that big lump asked the more I never thought I was never going to see day light again. Not only that, they knew far too much information and no one else had been pulled in, only us. There could be no other conclusion than there must be a rat in the camp. But who?

Finally, after around six hours or so they concluded the interview and told us we were free to go but with a warning to me and no doubt the other two as well; that they knew me and

Andy were responsible for this and that just because they were allowing us to leave didn't mean they were finished with us.

They also informed me that they had spent a long time out at the Cumbernauld office getting a very detailed description of me. Though at that stage I couldn't give two fucks about any of that, I just wanted out.

We were released at different times, first Andy, then Stacey, then me. We all knew to meet back up at Stacey's house anyway, so getting out at different times didn't mean shit.

When I got back I couldn't believe my eyes. All the blood was gone, the tape was down, and police had all left. It was like nothing had ever happened. Although one thing was missing, Soap. He had no doubt heard all about the fiasco with us all getting arrested and left the city for greener pastures. In case you are wondering, Soap is a made-up name of the boy involved. So, if by the crazy chance that there is in fact a boy called Soap in or around the area it's a total coincidence.

After getting back up the stairs to Stacey's house Andy came in and we both took the short walk to the shop. It gave us time to talk. To be honest I was keen to hear what they had said to him and was expecting the same response but to my surprise he was beyond pissed with me.

The first words out his mouth were, 'When did you go down and fucking stab him after we left?'

I was blown away. Did he honestly think that I had done this? Then the penny started to drop and right away I went straight on the defence:

'Here Andy, just wait two fucking seconds, I done fuck all to him. Ask Nikki she knows what I did and didn't do.'

'So who did?' His shoulders were still tense, his stance signifying that at any moment he could go off.

'Listen mate if you don't know, that's something you're going to have to work out for yourself. I'm no rat, not in there, not out here.' I watched with relief as his shoulders slumped and arms relaxed a little.

'Okay Paul, okay I still don't believe you, but I will investigate it myself in due time.' Then the atmosphere started to relax, and the conversation turned to more important questions like what did they ask you?

After drinking our weight in nectar we both concluded that we were solid and even agreed that there must have been a snitch in that house. Surprisingly we both came up with the same name. This would be the first time this individual name would come up as a rat, but it wouldn't be the last. We never could prove it even to this day, so I won't be naming the person's name. They know who they are and if their soul is stained that's something they will have to carry with them for the rest of their lives.

As the days ticked by without incident life just returned to normal. No one ever did get charged with what happened and I have kept Biscuit and Soap's real names, to myself for over twenty years now.

As for the boy that was stabbed, he pulled through with grace of God I might add and supposedly went on the hunt for those responsible. I was in Prison by that point and had other things on my mind.

Still, for years after the stabbing I was always amazed just how easily the polis gave up on it. Was Glasgow so violent that unless they could

guarantee a conviction, they would just sweep it under the rug? The small fact that most of Scotland's Prisons are around eighty percent Glaswegian pours cold water on that theory though.

I guess sometimes in life you all get lucky, the boy was lucky he pulled through, and we were lucky not to be taking a trip to the High Court. Not that day anyway.

BONNIE NIGHT (2001)

One thing in life you are guaranteed is karma, I believe that, even more so today than I ever have before. Why? Because I have filled my own karma bank over the years with both good and bad pennies; mostly bad with a sprinkle of good! When I have done a good deed virtually every time I get it returned to me ten times over.

One specific time that comes to mind, came on the night of November 5th - bonfire night or bonnie night depending what part of the country you're from. As all the kids and adults from the Cumbernauld area gathered, marveling at the crackling sounds coming from the bonnie with all its bright flashes from overpriced fireworks illuminating the night sky, I lay on the brink of death, feeling the cold concrete beneath me.

I was mere minutes away from my grave. Funny thing is, only ten minutes prior we were all dancing the night away in a house party one landing up.

The day in question started a whole lot different. Indeed, it didn't even start in the Cumbernauld area, it all began in Glasgow, which at the time was becoming my full-time address. I'd left Cumbernauld behind for the bright lights of Cranhill, a housing Scheme at the Eastend of the city that I had almost adopted as my own.

I can still remember every detail of that fateful day.

As teenagers in Scotland, you waited the full year for Halloween then Bonfire night and for me in November I also had my own birthday followed by the crème de la crème - the birthday of our lord and savior big Jesus C known to all as Christmas day.

All these dates stood out as memorable dates on the calendar. Kids would spend months collecting wood trying to outdo everyone else's bonnie. It seemed Cranhill was no different.

I spent most of that morning on the balcony of the old gray maisonette block of flats. The home of my first-born son Paul. His mother, a girl called Stacey Lennox - not to be mixed up with my fiancée Stacey Rice around whom I have built my life.

I stood there watching kids of all ages running up and down the street laden with wooden doors, big pallets, and sheets of OSB - the sheets of wood used to fit over smashed windows, and basically anything else that they could on burn that one night of the year.

The smart ones would have their wheelie bins under lock and key. Better that than waking up the following morning to find nothing more than a charred black spot from where your bin used to be.

Even from the crack of dawn that day there was a gut feeling telling me not to be in Cumbernauld. Truth be told I was looking forward to witnessing for myself how the youth of Cranhill did their bonfires. For weeks I had been hearing stories about how they did the most amazing bonnies you had ever seen. So come November 5th I was buzzing to see this for myself. This fantastic looking fire came with a warning though, and this time it came not only from Stacey Lennox but also her brother Andy. The warning was simple enough - be careful.

I learned that every year, without fail, someone gets stabbed at the bonnie. If the information had only come from Stacey I would have just dismissed it; she had a wee problem with telling the truth. Here was also Cotton Candy (Andy) saying it too. So now I'm thinking *'Fuck, this could be legit. I'm keeping my head on a swivel tonight. No bastard's stabbing me.'*

As the morning turned into afternoon everyone started to ask if I had sweets (ecto's) on me. This was, after all, not only bonfire night but also the weekend. Cocaine just hadn't been heard of at that point.

We had two types of uppers' – sweets or speed. If you wanted to get high back then these were your choices. At least with the ecto's you could sleep the next day. I knew my supply was low and that I would probably need to tie in with my man to re-up.

I had no choice, I had to go back to Cumbernauld but didn't intend staying long, just a quick in and out, boom-boom and back to Glasgow.

So, I phoned my man and gave him the heads-up and to my surprise he was coming into the city anyway, his job had him driving a lot so that was a wee result for me.

Twenty minutes later he beeped the horn. I jumped down to his motor to meet him. So, there I was, sitting with a fist full of dollars getting ready to give him his paper in exchange for a big fucking party in a bag. In short, there were enough disco biscuits in that bag to have all the young teams of Glasgow out in the street dancing to car alarms. So, there we were, just two guys, well a full-grown man and a young boy sitting in a car talking away without a care in the world with the police driving past us every few minutes.

Easterhouse police station was just a few miles up the road and Bellrock Street, what you would call a high-risk crime area wasn't far off. So, seeing police patrolling in that area was no big deal, most people didn't even look up.

I found myself sitting in a car with a bag of pills watching all these polis driving past thinking to myself, *God, if one of them turned their head just an inch we'd be fucked.*

To be honest it made me feel notorious, like a young Pablo. Every nano-second of my little fantasy was pure nonsense of course, but to a sixteen-year-old drunk on his own so-called success, it felt like, *'Fuck me I've went from being a piss ant no one in Cumbernauld to selling drugs in one of the roughest schemes in Glasgow'*

After that it became hard even trying to keep my feet on the ground. It's strange to think of how I was back then.

As for the guy I was sitting beside in the car that afternoon, within just three short months I would be involved in almost taking his life. It's strange just how fast shit can spin out of control on the street sometimes - whether you want it to or not.

But for the time being we were making money together and even becoming friends. Fuck the age difference, we were becoming close and before your mind goes to that dirty place, we were just drug dealing friends. Not the fucking Michael Jackson and Macaulay Culkin kind of friends.

So as our conversation ended, I paid my dues and was off on my merry way. I walked up to my stash - a hiding spot only I knew about. I mean all these guys were my friends and all, but they were also a bunch of pirates that would rob you blind. A lesson I was to learn all too well a few months later when two of my so-called amigos robbed a full tub of blue diazepam tablets from me while I was incarcerated on my big one.

Anyway, that shit was almost a year away still and honestly, compared to the trouble I still had ahead of me, it was minimal. Not that I ever forgot about it, just put it down to being part and parcel of street guy life; nothing I wouldn't have done to them.

Back to the stash on that bonfire afternoon, I took out around thirty or so and went to do my rounds. I would always try giving a free one or two to a wee lassie called Charlie, she was a complete knock-out but was going out with some wee guy from another scheme. I can't remember the boy's name. Then again, I didn't give two fucks about him anyway. If I had ever gotten the chance, I would have been right in there. I say that now but honestly at the time I was just too scared to say anything to her. My confidence waned especially when trying to talk to a girl.

I guess back then I was always trying to build up the courage to just walk over to her and slap her on the arse and say look what you could be getting you lucky thing! Unfortunately, I never did, I just sat on the side lines and watched her pass me by. Fuck it! Such is life.

Going back to the bonnie night. It must have been around five pm by the time I finished my rounds. Everyone was starting to crack open their wine and wash back the pills from my little bag of tricks - everyone but me. I had been so busy doing my drops I hadn't had the chance to even spark a can of Stella. And I still had to take out a good chunk of them to meet a guy I will just call Stingray. He had stopped fucking about in Cranhill by then and decided he was going back to the sunny streets of Cumbernauld.

All I needed that night was just ten short minutes to myself - just ten minutes to sort my shit out and I was golden. My phone just wouldn't shut-the-fuck-up and before I knew it, night had fallen upon us. When I looked at the time it was close to nine pm and I was by then already half cut. My phone continued buzzing; it seemed like half of Cumbernauld wanted to get fucked up on pills. And no one else had any bar me. This was anything but true.

People can say what they like about Stingray, that boy moved more of my pills in a night than I could in a week. He was a 100% worker bee, buzzing from one scheme to another, getting shit done. Back then, for me, this was fantastic. It gave me more time with Kelly, my girlfriend at the time. Plus, to be honest I was never one for the limelight anyway.

Whereas Stingray, well what can I say, he had an ego bigger than the Empire State to quote Frankie De Chico. He loved the spotlight, loved selling sweets, loved meeting people, especially ones on buses for some mad reason. And was good at bringing home the paper. So, if there was one person on this earth I had to meet that night it was him.

Unfortunately, though, after a serious situation happened to him in Cranhill he refused to come back through. I down blame him mind you, but it did make shit more difficult in the beginning. Eventually it made more sense to spit the pills almost right down the middle; him in Cumbernauld me in Cranhill. Then there were two of us out there covering both areas. All I had to do was one simple thing, tie in with him, give him the sweets and I could enjoy the fireworks.

Only he wasn't coming near Cranhill, and I wasn't about to be going into the city centre with a pocket full of Saturday night specials.

So, there was no choice, I had to go back to my old homeland, only I still had that odd feeling. I can't even to this day describe it, I just knew something was off. Like always though, greed gets the better of you. so, after going over to the Cranhill bonnie we all headed through. Around ten of us or so, everyone boozed up looking for a good time.

We all headed for Seafar to meet Stingray, hand him some jolly rogers so to speak. By the time we got there we were on the other side of ten o-clock. Good thing for me was that for everyone there the night was just beginning. No one cared that this was me just turning up.

There was still definitely a problem, and it was a big one. Me and Kelly. I still cared for her and me turning up in Cumbernauld with Stacey Lennox of all people was just out of order. So, the faster I could get out of Seafar the better.

But what could I do? I had to meet Stingray and I knew Kelly would probably be there and I couldn't take this big crowd down with me either.

Anyway, if the shoe was on the other foot and I was to arrive in the middle of the night with a crowd of others to see Stingray after what happened in Glasgow, I would see that as a set up. So, I decided, best I go alone.

I was standing in the middle of the street pondering what to do with all these Glasgow refugees running wild in bandit country when my mobile rang - it none other than my old mate the blonde one.

Jackpot, I thought. I can have them sit in her house until I've done what I came here to do then we can all get the hell out of Dodge.

I was away maybe a half an hour with Stingray; gave him what I needed to give him, said my hello's, and left. I was even starting to feel like a stranger in my own scheme. That has never left me as I never have truly attached myself to anywhere in Cumbernauld since. Even now, I still plan to move back to Glasgow one day.

So, around eleven that night the crowd made their way to the blonde one's house. Her man wasn't much for party's and the posse were having fun being out of Glasgow for the night.

Yet, that feeling of doom I had been having all day was not replaced with euphoria and happiness from all the pills and cans of Stella we had been consuming. Then a wee lassie called Rosie appeared and told everyone that we could move the party over to her flat. It wasn't too far, just one scheme away.

This decision almost cost me my life.

At some point my cousin Caroline and her boyfriend Stew appeared, why I can't say, but I just thought, the more the merrier. It had all the makings of a good night out – well, apart from the small fact I had to listen to Caroline's shite about some of the people I was running about with. She was never very keen on Stacey Lennox, even in the beginning.

I can't remember the reason why, but everyone got into taxis and me and big Stew McGlocklin walked over to the new party venue. I think it may have had something to do with my inability to travel in cars full of pills without being sick. Whatever the reason we joked about all the fun times we had before I fucked off to Glasgow and even he had gone his own way. By then, he and my cousin were running with each other full time and never running with any of the old crew.

What happened next seemed like something straight out of a Chevy Chase movie. The crew had gone on ahead with the Blonde One, Caroline, Greg, and wee Rosie only to find that Rosie had left the keys behind. Now this was a small problem, the smart thing to do would be to send someone back to get them. Instead, a pissed as a fart Rosie tells Big Harry to kick the door in.

Now Harry was a bit of a lump of a boy to say the least, he not only kicked in the door, he kicked it either just right or that hard the whole door came off the hinges and just fell in.

At this point most people would think, *'Right, fuck this. Party's over, everyone needs to go somewhere else,'* and phone a joiner. However, all these fucking lunatics start piling into the house and when the last was in, big Harry simply picked up the door, fitted it back into the frame and joined the rest of the revelers in the living room.

A small time later me and Big Stew appeared - even from bottom of the close you could hear the music blasting. So, by the time we got upstairs to her door it was deafening. No way were they going to hear a simple chap. So Stew gives it one big bang and the whole door caves in. We just stood there in pure shock for a half a second then hit the floor in hysterics. Remember we knew nothing about the door getting kicked in, as far as we knew Big Stew was fucking Herman Munster who had taken the door right out it's frame.

The rest of the night wasn't to be so much fun.

KARMA'S A BITCH

Two hours on, one of the crew, Neil suggested a walk up to the ASDA on the opposite side of the bridge from where the house was, so me and him and my brother Craig left. We laughed and joked as we went down the stairs but that was all.

There is a story out there that we, for no apparent reason, started kicking this guy's door in. I mean come on, why would we start kicking someone's door in at two in the morning for no reason? Total nonsense.

What happened was the three of us came down the staircase, on the bottom step I slip off, putting my hand out to break the fall and hit his door by pure accident. It didn't even make a bang big enough to wake him up. Then on we went.

By the time we hit the bridge only a few steps away, him and his dad where out shouting my name. I wondered why these pricks were shouting at me. I hated him, everyone in Cumbernauld hated him. For years there had been rumours going around about him being a beast with shit involving kids - though I don't honestly know if this was true or not. I might hate the ball licking bastard, but I don't believe in jumping on the band wagon because everyone else is. I just didn't like him regardless.

So, for him to be shouting me at 2am only meant trouble. I pulled out my lockback and ran back. When I got there, his dad jumped in front of him. This was one fat bastard of a man, like Eddie Murphy in the Nutty Professor, fat, and he's standing there with a half-sized pirate sword and there I am with a daft wee lockback in my hand. Believe me guys, in situations like this size matters. What could I do? I was already running back down the hill from the bridge with Neil and my brother fast on my heels.

As soon as I got to him I didn't flinch, didn't blink - just stabbed my knife into his chest. I buried it so deep in his torso the knife wouldn't come back out. Then I knew I was in trouble. I knew that wee prick had a lockback and I'd just stabbed his old man. Talk about giving someone incentive. Low and behold the inevitable happened. At first I thought he punched me in the stomach. I remember thinking to myself, *'What a stupid thing to do. I've just stabbed your dad and that's your come back?'*

Then I saw the blood. In that instant my whole life changed. Shock took over. My legs gave way. He got me good to say the least. I flopped to the pavement, blood spraying out of me like a fire hydrant. The pair of them rained their knives down on me and stabbed me a few more times.

Had it not been for my guardian angel Neil Lennox I would have died for sure. He ran at them getting in a few punches while the youngest of the two continued kicking into me. Neil ended up getting stabbed a few times around the ear and head. Nothing major, cuts mostly.

At some point during all this madness one of my mates must have looked out the window and saw all the commotion. All hell broke loose and everyone came running. It was a mad scramble. The police had the same notion and six maybe seven officers appeared to find ten of my mates all wielding machetes and kitchen knives, the entire Maguire family, including the mum and sister all having a mass brawl in the middle of a block of flats. And during all that I lay dying.

The police could do nothing but attempt to fight my mates back until finally they circled the family to protect them. I mean what else could they do? I had family and friends and every one of them wanted blood.

Like I said. the coldness of death was starting to set in. All I could do was look up at the multiple police officers faces who by then, were frantically radioing for an ambulance so I knew it was bad.

It was weird, every time I looked up my surroundings changed. One minute it was chaos then the next, people where in handcuffs, then my mother, and stepfather were there. My mother was frantic – she could see her son dying before her very eyes. I could hear her wailing, her raised voice screaming, 'my boy, my boy. He's dying. Please, someone save him. Do something.'

To this day, I don't know who phoned my mother. One of the girls? My cousin Caroline probably.

To me it seemed like I kept blinking my eyes and every time I blinked, things changed...What I learned later was that I had been drifting in and out of consciousness a few minutes at a time.

Neil was lying beside me trying to keep me awake asking me about my hero Henrik Larsson, for a good protestant boy like him it must have stung like a motherfucker, but he was doing everything in his power to keep me awake, keep me breathing. The boy did save my life that night. Well, him and the hospital.

My mother, on the other hand, kept me awake in her own way; bearhugging me and shouting, 'Who fucking done this?' She didn't realise the pain I was in even though she was hugging me so hard. Inadvertently she was putting me in even more pain. I mean, *Come on Angie!* But that was her, very protective as any mother should be I suppose.

Finally, the paramedics arrived. Unfortunately for me they could only park on the other side of the barrier, so a gurney was out of the question. The two paramedics weren't what you would call big built either. The guy was not exactly in his prime and the younger of the two, a wee lassie, maybe twenty-five or so wasn't lifting me, not in a month of Sundays. Thankfully, because of the riot that had kicked off the Cumbernauld Police office had sent out their biggest guys.

This big lump took over telling the paramedics, 'Don't worry guys, I've got him.' And in one swoop he's got me in his arms and running. Every step caused me severe pain, by now the blood is hemorrhaging out of me. I remember nothing about the ambulance ride to the hospital. Perhaps I passed out, I don't know. When I came to shocked and dazed, I was in Monklands Hospital getting wheeled down to the operating theatre. Again, it all went black.

I awoke the following morning to find I had very large scar running up my stomach which was being held together with staples. The pain was horrendous even with the morphine. I lay there with tubes coming out of me and a button in my hand what dispensed morphine every five minutes - that part of it wasn't so bad mind you. All I did was press the little blue button and all my problems just drifted away. It is one hell of a drug.

At some point in the morning the family started to arrive. First into the ward was Alex. I never knew just how bad a kicking I had taken, my face had that much swelling he didn't even recognize me at first. Then my mother, brother, auntie, uncle, and cousin with her man and, finally, Stacey. All of them stood around my bed cursing and swearing, calling the Maguires for everything and vowing revenge.

I was that high their words were just bouncing off me; none of it was sinking in. I was sore and weak and very tired. All I wanted was for them to go. I understood why their emotions where high but to me at that moment in time I was feeling low and just wanted to be left alone. I was far from making much sense anyway. I was in and out of sleep and high as kite when I was up and awake, my train of thought was pure gobbledygook.

Finally, the visit ended, everyone left and my long road to recovery began. The pain was getting worse hour by hour, clearly something bad was going on. My stomach had a continual sharp pain, even with the morphine nothing shifted it. As the days ticked by, I was moved from high dependency to a run of the mill ward. The nursing staff were bastards. I'm sorry to even say that but this is me talking nice about them.

It all came to a head around the fifth day. After a few hours of lying in severe pain a doctor finally came around and felt around my scar. The news was far from encouraging. I was told that I may need to go back under the knife. More surgery? You've got to be kidding! Is there no other option? All I was told was that a discussion would be held to consider potential outcomes regarding another operation.

The news only added to my low mood. The first three or four days in there had been hard, not only from the pain, which was bad enough, but also all the thoughts as to why I was lying there in the first place. I don't just mean the knife wound but also the life I was living and more importantly, did I still want to be involved in it anymore? The answer was 'definitely not.'

However, it wasn't all doom and gloom, my good friend and next-door neighbour was coming up that night. Big Martin stayed next door but ran with different guys. So, the fact that he was making the effort to come up made me feel good and upbeat.

Around six o'clock the visit started. Right on time in he walked bringing with him grapes, juice and, as a joke, a wee dirty mag to help me pass the time. Out of nowhere I started being violently sick. It was coming from everywhere, right in front of a packed visit. Talk about embarrassing, but what could I do? It just wouldn't stop. Then this smug bitch of a nurse came running in and pulled the curtains around the bed. Instead of getting in a doctor she slammed down a carboard sick cup along with a warning that if I did that again during a visit she would cancel my visit and tell my people to leave. Are you fucking kidding me on? By that stage the sickness was over, and anger was now fueling me.

'Fuck this, Martin, help me get dressed. I'm fucking out of here.' Suddenly this horrible bitch turned white and was trying to calm me down because she could see I was serious. She had no choice, she had to bring in a doctor.

A small man in a white coat arrived and tried his hardest to sound aggressive, demanding I get back into bed - a bed soaked in sick I might add, or they would restrain me if necessary.

I was thinking, *what the fuck is happening here? Who the hell do these halfwit's think they are*? It turned out the doctor was right, especially if you're in danger of losing your life they have the right to detain you, so I was snookered. If they thought I was about to get back into that bed they had another thing coming.

Before I could say anything more Martin started piping up, his voice rising higher and higher and just as they got Martin to simmer down everyone else in the ward, patients and visitors alike started putting their two cents worth. I was over the moon with them all. The whole ward all up in arms backing up little old me. Honestly if I wasn't sore, I would have been leading the revolution, small as it was. Or, at the very least, I would have been stirring the pot. All I could do was get back into bed and beg for some painkillers. Even those few minutes out of bed killed me.

I had to admit maybe they were right. Maybe me trying to impersonate Papillon and escape Monklands Hospital was bad idea.

Finally, after nine days, I was getting released. I don't think I have ever been happier than I was that day.

My release from hospital wasn't exactly straight forward. Yes, I was to be discharged but given I was considered fit enough to go home it gave the police license to come and interview me. The police were coming up in the lift to interview me now that I was deemed heathy enough to see them.

I was devastated, there I was having just spent nine days in the hospital and on the brink of release only to be arrested on my way out the door. What could I do? I couldn't run anywhere; I could barely walk. I had no option but to see what they wanted.

I had no idea that they were coming up to charge me with stabbing his fat fuck of a father. I was shell shocked when they started the conversation with a caution, then within a mere few words went on to formally charge me and put me in handcuffs. It was laughable, I was barely able to stand up right and still they handcuffed me. They did, however, tell me, 'You're in luck lad. Our sergeant has told us to just take you straight to court.' So, I bypassed yet another horrible day and night in the cells. There was still a very strong chance of being remanded to prison and I needed that like I needed a fucking hole in the head.

Finally, we got to Airdrie Sheriff Court. I was that weak I found it hard to even make it up to the Dock. If anything, that went in my favour, the Sheriff told both me and my Lawyer that if I was fit enough, I was heading for Barlinnie that very day. Due to my right to seek the best medical care, he had no choice but to release me on bail. After what felt like months not days, I saw the Cumbernauld skyline once more.

AFTERMATH (2001)

We were lucky to have been home ten minutes when my so-called promises of turning over that new leaf were all but gone.

I had one thing on my mind, hitting the street and tying in with the lads. I was keen show off my scars, pathetic I now know, but what I can say? When you're sixteen, bragging rights are intertwined with most of your day-to-day activities. After sneakily texting Jay to chap the door, I told my mother I was thinking I would go out for a quick walk to get some fresh air. All bullshit of course. She knew; she was far from daft, after all she had been listening to my shite my entire life. Even before the stabbing her attempts at trying to keep my ass in the house, even for my own safety or as a punishment, were ineffective to say the least. Now I had turned sixteen and was old enough to do what I liked, well, she was shit-out-of-luck and we both knew it.

By the time Jay banged the door she just gave in, passed me some money, and told me, 'Make sure no drinking Paul and,' it went without saying, 'stay out of trouble.'

All her words, I'm sorry to say, fell on deaf ears. Soon as I was out that door, I was right back to my old ways straight up to the Off sales for a bottle of black Tar, known more commonly as Buckfast. Still, as I stood there, I was privately making promises with myself, stuff like: *Today I will only be drinking one bottle just to celebrate pulling through to show my appreciation of life.*

I'll stay sober the rest of the week. No drugs, no matter what, for the foreseeable future. And if the polis come? I'm just walking away, allow all my mates, the same ones that couldn't even be arsed taking a trip up to the hospital for a visit I might add, to take the old stop and search for a change.

By this stage I was getting sick of the none stop polis harassment anyway. Unfortunately, my promises and determination to stop walking on the wild side were anything but. All my good intentions didn't even last the week.

I was never a bad kid, that's the truth. I just made bad decisions, no doubt about it. A bad person, that's not the case - perhaps a little bit of an attention seeker that's all.

As soon as I heard the cheer go up from all the boys, I got buoyed up from all that attention. Getting the chance to show off the scars was just the cherry on the cake. So all my previous decisions just drifted out the window. There was nothing quite like getting some of the limelight - all that attention and sympathy. It made my head swell. That was it. I hadn't even made it through the day and already I was back drinking like a fish, hanging around with the boys figuring out how to get back at those bastards.

We had heard through the grapevine that only his son got charged and not the his old man but without my statement, his lawyer would have already told him 'not to worry, chances are those charges will probably just go away. Which is exactly what happened I may add. The only justice I wanted was street justice, plain and simple.

We all spent that night running through one scenario after another with one common theme in mind, vengeance. Some of the ideas where just pure street talk; a gang of teens talking tough. Some suggestions did have legs, but most were nothing more than bravado.

One thing that was a must was returning the favour. There had to be pay-back for what they had done, plus the fact that the pair of them where two dirty, grassing, bastards. It had to happen.

I wanted, even needed, to plug him personally for my own sanity - which wasn't the best then I have to say. When the time came could I go through with it?

Physically I was damaged, no doubt there, but psychologically, that was something very different. There was real damage done, the sort of damage that would take years to come to the surface. All I knew was at that moment in time was that something had changed and within myself I felt markedly different.

Still, that cocksucker had to feel some pain. My pride had been hurt and my reputation. Getting stabbed off that wanker ... I mean him of all people, come on Paul! Get it together man. It was a huge embarrassment to say the least.

After a few days of all the talk, which was honestly going nowhere, I put it on the back burner and headed back into Glasgow to run with the wolves again.

By this point I felt well enough to stand up straight and move around more freely. Being bed-bound for two weeks, stuck lying in that fucking hospital was worse than prison. Now there is a fact I will standby. Anyway, I was finally starting to get back to full strength.

A knife wound to the abdomen leaves you struggling to straighten up and walk right. I had spent those past few weeks taking almost baby steps, being unable to get my body into an upright position was a challenge to say the least. As the days ticked by more and more I was becoming more like my old self. I was by then starting to miss all the troops, especially Nikki. She was without doubt my best female friend. In fact, I would go even further than that and say she was the closest thing I've ever had to a sister, that's how tight we were at the time.

Reflecting on the feelings inside me - there was definitely something different. That kind of hurt had planted some strange feelings. I now felt something I had never felt before, it was a feeling of pure nothingness – my emotional bank was empty. Not a very nice place to be let me tell you.

It was a pure aggression and hate that ran through my blood, but as for any other emotions I'm sorry to say there were zero. No happiness, no joy, no fear, no hope. Pure nothingness.

Previously I was this fun loving happy go lucky wee guy who loved life, but now there was nothing but hollowness.

I was severely starting to snap, I was taking every wee comment personally, jokes were lost on me, a coldness came across me which was reflected in the way others reacted to me. I'd lost that fun loving innocence that probably attracted people to me in the first place. All that remained was an angry and dangerous young teen who was willing to stab anyone and everyone and wasn't afraid of death and far from afraid to kill.

Stabbing people was nothing new it was something we had all done in the past but now I was almost looking for a reason to hurt someone. Before this though, I would do what I felt had to be done. I never got any pleasure from violence; it was more like a means to an end. Boys like Jay would do it and you could almost see the child-like glee in his eyes. I used think, you're a fucking barbarian mate.

Now though, something had cracked inside me, I had become almost determined to take another man's life. I realise today just how sick this is but at the time I was in a very different place emotionally and mentally.

Without even realizing it I was dragging everyone else into my misery. Nobody wanted to be around me. Gradually I watched people walk away, one by one they left. I didn't even blame them. I could see the things I was doing and the way I was acting was wrong, but I couldn't stop myself. It was as though I was observing it all looking through another man's eyes.

Even me and Jay were starting to bump heads - how the hell all of that started I don't know. Perhaps he thought I was somehow involved in him getting stabbed. Total fucking lies. I had nothing to do with it.

No matter the reason, we managed to fuck up a very close friendship but that's how that summer ended. A real shame if you ask me.

The beginning of that Summer was very different. We were all thick as thieves and best of friends. Me and Jay, John, Duncan, Ginger, Kelly, Jamie, Robert Foye was even coming down not to mention all the rest of the troops. We were stuck together day in day out loving every moment of it. Fuck, we even had a wee gay mascot, called Robert or pink pants as he we more commonly knew him. He might have had more of an eye for the Stephen's than the Stacey's of the group if you get my drift, but he was one of the best wee guys you could ever find.

Him and his mate Jimmy Lenny would come over from time to time. We even went out with them one-night to a gay bar and honestly what a laugh we had. At the beginning of the night there were about seven of us, all with our arses almost tattooed against the wall. All debating who had the balls to go to the bar. 'Who's going to man up and walk through this big bunch of flamboyant men and women?'

Then the ecstasy kicked in with all of us. I even remember the brand of pill we took: green speckled shamrocks - and that was it, all of us taking control of the dance floor having the laugh of our lives, kidding them all on that we were regulars. I won't name the names of the other boys but believe me what a giggle. Ecstasy was one hell of drug. Everyone there probably knew we were all straight because no one tried their luck or maybe the fact we were all smashed on sweets and looking and acting like out-of-control visitors from another planet might have been a contributing factor, who knows?

Not that we were looking...

I believe, the real reason we all had such a good time is that unlike a normal dancing place there was no violence at any time whatsoever. When it came to closing time everyone just got into their taxis, buses and cars and off they went.

That was probably the last time I was out for night out without some sort of violence happening to me, from me, or around me.

Still, away from all the bullshit, money was still coming in every week from the party pills. Though even that would get fucked up. Over time I manage to fuck everything up. Why? Who honestly knows? However, it should be noted that not every act of violence was someone getting stabbed.

Around about that time I was also swallowing handfuls of uppers downers and round and rounders. I was severely tumbling down the rabbit hole to the point even my friends in Glasgow were starting to take notice. Nothing mattered anymore apart from causing chaos.

On top of all that, there was a girl out there telling people that her new-born baby Dean was mine. She was generous with her attentions with all the boys, no doubt about that, and there was a small chance that another one of the troops could be responsible - but deep down I always knew he was mine. To this day I've always regretted turning my back on my own child. The truth is I was scared and too immature, wrapped up in all my own shite to care. Plus, by then I was fast tracking towards prison, already on bail for two inditements that could themselves take me to the High Court but instead of lying low, I found myself running about gang fighting for Cranhill.

I wasn't even from that city and there I was risking my life fighting a scheme I had never even been in before and for what? I mean we were going hard at it with this mob in Glasgow called Ruchazie - almost every night, gang fighting on the adjoining bridge running across the M80 Motorway. Now that was terrifying, okay it was 98% shouting and launching bottles and bricks at one another. Every so often one side or the other would lead the cavalry charge and all hell would break out.

And why did I get mixed up in that mess? Again, who the hell knows? I will never know why and I doubt anyone else will either. Hey-ho. I will say this, fighting on that bridge was the most terrifying experience of my life. The fear that someone might stab, slash, chop or even, God-forbid, fling your ass off the railings and onto the road below, even today if I'm ever passing it in a car a chill runs down my spine.

So, there I was a father and a fuck up all round. Even if I had been in Dean's life in the beginning, I would have been a disaster. I was nothing more than a half-pissed, half-doped up ned only in it for himself, so the wee man was better off not knowing me. That much I did know. I mean, I was sixteen years old, out running wild around a scheme full of headcases where violence was ingrained in everyday life, and I was there, right in the middle it.

Two things were to happen that would forever etch my name on the minds of Easterhouse Police. One, I was involved in. The other, I was merely standing watching it unfold.

BAD REPUTATION'S STICK

The first to happen was me giving a boy called Paul the kicking of his life. Even I will admit I went too far with this one - he had it coming, no two ways about it. Everything started on a Friday night outside the phone box. There was me, Stacey, and my secret crush Charlie. As the two lassies gabbed away outside the box I spoke with Jay inside on the telephone getting filled in on the escapades through our way, nothing big just hello goodbye.

As I exited the box, along came this boy called Paul with that boozed-up, looking-for-a-fight look in his eyes. Normally I would be only too happy to comply, but on that night, all I wanted to do was unwind, take some pills, have a booze, and spend the rest of the night taking crap to my mate Nikki. This boy had different ideas. He came over and purposely cut in front of me, to the point I had to step off the pavement and onto the road. 'Okay,' I'm thinking to myself. *'Guy's a clown trying to flex his skinny ass muscles in front of a pair of teenage girls.'* I guess we've all done that. So, at that point I'm still just laughing to myself thinking, *mate you look like a fanny standing there.*

Then he puts his whole hand onto Stacey's face and pushes her, while at the exact same time slapping Charlie. The story to this day is I kicked his head off every wall in Cranhill because he hit Stacey, but the real reason was to impress wee Cha-Cha. That is how it played out from start to finish.

He went around telling people that I hit him with a bottle, again this is only partly true. I did hit him with a bottle. A plastic bottle, a half empty plastic bottle I might add. I swung it, catching him on the left eye and taking him to him knees. I guess he thought it was a wine bottle, that's Bucky not Rose, and he instantaneously just fell on his arse. Then, I'm sorry to say, I never let him back to his feet. The beating I gave him was so severe I had no doubt in my mind he would die or not last the night.

At the time I couldn't have cared less. It makes me sick now, to think how much of a messed-up mind I must have had, but in that moment all I wanted to do was impress wee Charlie so that she would look up and think, 'Where has your sexy arse been all my life?' In fact, it did the opposite, before she didn't even know I existed, now she knew me for kicking the living shit out one of her best pals. Right smooth Paul!

Instead of just going up to her and asking her out I show her how much of an alpha male I was by knocking fuck out this boy only to find out they grew up together. I doubt I would ever have had a chance with her anyway, just one of those things, best to brush yourself off and move on.

In the following days I was on the people's radar. Him and his mate were allegedly out on the hunt for me. Perhaps they were. It made sense he wouldn't take it lying down. No pun intended.

Around this time I also heard that Easterhouse Police also wanted to talk with me. About what I didn't know. I was given to understand that Paul never said anything, so who did?

Was there someone out there ratting?

Was it someone within my own camp?

Suspicion wouldn't start to point at one individual until the another incident that followed this not long after. Now this was where the real danger lay, mostly because I was about to be charged with murder for something I had only a minor involvement with at best.

KID-ON CAR THIEVES

The year was almost at an end. The laugher becoming less and less. The hangovers more frequent and the level of friends was just above the zero mark. This was where I was at a mere eighteen months along after the bells had rung to welcome in the start of the millennium.

"and I was causing myself enough trouble to last me until the next millennium"

Despite being just sixteen years old at the time I could see the good times were over.

I had become somewhat disillusioned with myself by then. Everything I thought I wanted in life turned out not to be true.

Had I turned a corner? Was it too late? These were all questions that rattled around in my mind, sometimes on a daily occurrence. I wanted a normal job; I wanted a normal life. Perhaps one day even a wife. The job and life part anyway. I wanted the chance to enjoy all the good things that people usually take for granted. Even though I knew there was nothing out there stopping me from getting them, simply reaching out and grabbing them presented itself as a huge challenge. I would use excuses like my dyslexia and how that was stopping me achieving the things I wanted to do in life. It was all complete nonsense but somehow, I had convinced myself, wrapped myself up in my own false perceptions. I felt trapped in a prison of my own making. The prospect of continually going in and out of prison like a revolving door year after year looked like hell. I knew it was probably too late. I knew that the crimes

I had already committed were sure to result in jail time. There was no escape, I had to pay the piper.

The thoughts I was having weren't due to a fear of prison more the dawning of the sad realisation that I would wake up one morning only to realise my life had been wasted and I was nothing more than a sad shell of an old man with an extensive prison record under his belt.

I had to stand up and pay the price with my liberty for the things I had done, this fact I knew all too well. Paying for it for the rest of life. That sounded onerous to say the least.

Finally, for the first time in a long time I opened my eyes just enough to fully see what I had become. A liar, a half-drunk, with a bunch of thieves and back-stabbing bastards as friends. Was I any better? Probably not!

It became a daily grind, waking hungover, looking for money to spend on more drink and fags, silly distractions and yet there was always that oblique hope that today would be better than the last. It never was.

I realised it wasn't a life. It was a horrible existence and honestly, that's all it was. The existence of drink, drugs and lose woman.

I felt dizzy with it all. I wanted off that hell of a merry go round but questioned whether it was possible? Could I just walk away? Was it that easy? What was even stopping me? People had done it in the past. Plenty of people in fact. Then it hit home that the only thing stopping me was me. Me and my own fears that was it, pure and simple. I wanted off. I wanted away. I wanted a new life. Yet I was just too scared to just reach out and grab it. I was too scared to hope.

Of course, there are people out there, many people who would question this and possibly claim that I was generally the one encouraging all the madness. That I was the one who went out looking for it and yes, for a time anyway, it was true. I did. I will not stand here and say I was some sort of saint because believe me I was anything but. I was just as guilty of instigating situations as the next person but by this stage in life I had truly become sickened with it all. How much violence could there be before it was my number that was up? How much time would I get when the shit hits the fan? Eventually everyone gets caught, it was inevitable and my card had been well and truly marked already. My decision to walk away may have been my smartest one yet. It suddenly made sense more than ever before.

One of the problems with getting involved in something dodgy is that you usually tend to be neck deep in it before you open your eyes and realise it's not for you. I remember sometimes spending full days considering this topic, wanting desperately to fling my hands up and say 'fuck this shit I'm done.' Then all it would take was someone to suggest a thrill-seeking idea and on impulse I was on board forgetting all those thoughts that been clouding my mind. It didn't matter what it was, but mostly it amounted to showing off – and why?

On reflection I believe it was the only medium through which I found a sense of status and self-confidence, or so I thought. My reputation was built on recklessness. I was always one of the first to volunteer; albeit the theft of a motor, or stabbing someone, or just general anti-social behaviour.

No matter what it was, I was always game, and no sooner it was over I was back to feeling frustrated and wrestling with my conscience and emotions.

By the end of the summer when the nights were getting just that little bit colder these thoughts were becoming increasingly more urgent, yet it did nothing to spoil the mood.

Everyone was still hanging around at the back of Stacey's block of maisonette style flats, congregating on her landing all times of the day. Herr's was the place everyone gravitated to especially on a Friday with the excitement of the weekend coming up.

I saw the writing on the wall, people splintering away when they saw me coming up the street. I knew people were all getting sick of me. To them I was an unpredictable, volatile teenager with something to prove and who could blame them? Not that anyone said anything, it was more a case of being polite than fear I believe.

Of course, no one knew of my thinking at this time. No one knew it was me that wanted to change! I wasn't exactly big on sharing; quietly thinking of a straight life going through my mind day after day.

Yet my thrill-seeking drive was out of control. Just one word from my mate and hay-ho away we went. One incident comes to mind. It was after a night of yet more drinking when Gibby happened to mention how good a driver he was. That small push from Gibby was all it took. I was compelled by the thrill of going out there and then and stealing a car. I don't even believe he mentioned anything about stealing. I took the idea and ran with it, pulling everyone else along with me.

I started to bare face lie to him, telling him,

'Don't worry bro I know all about stealing cars,' complete lies on my part. To a sixteen-year-old show off a wee white lie wasn't the end of the world.

Growing up back home car thieves were ten a penny and the king of the stolen cars without a doubt was Robert Foye. His record was horrendous, by far surpassing everyone else. He was also the best person to teach you too.

At some early point in my ned career Foye tried showing me how to break into cars, even start them up. Doing it myself. Never! The closest I ever got was watching him from the passenger seat. Then suddenly, there I was out with Gibby with a five-millimeter screwdriver in hand on the hunt for a car to take for the night.

All we needed to do was chose a car, mess about with the lock, rip off the casing, start it up and off we'd go.. It seemed simple enough in principle. What could go wrong? The plan was that I would break into the car start it up then Gibby would take control with both of us driving off unnoticed.

Now this was a trick even I would be surprised to see go to plan. There was still that small but significant point - I knew nothing about stealing cars!

Fuck it, I decided we will take a crack at it anyway. So, with that the two of us set out walking down Bellrock Street. We both agreed that neither of us would touch any cars in the Riddrie area. Not for fear of getting caught, nothing like that. It was more to do with the fact that most of the staff from Barlinnie prison bought their houses in this scheme and we ran the very serious risk of stealing one of their cars - then you're stuck in prison with them. You can only imagine the treatment we would receive.

The rumour about the prison staff moving into the Riddrie estate all started around the late '70's, so I'm told. It had something to do with them getting their homes on the cheap. Supposedly back then. the powers that be thought, *if we help buy them their homes all our staff will be in and around the surrounding areas of the prison. Then they can all jump out of bed, clickety-click, in the middle of the night if, God forbid, something kicks off like a wee riot.* That way they would have all their eggs in one basket.

Now, we didn't quite pinch one of *their* cars, but we did manage to get caught in a screws sister's car. after wrapping it into the side of the Vogue Bingo Hall. How did this happen?

It was a case of pure laziness. Halfway down the street we became somewhat tired and were regretting our decision to leave Stacey's flat in the first place. Then, right in front of us was an old gray coloured shit box.

Thank God, I thought, *even I should be able to screw the lock on this* and off we went. Gibby kept a look out while I jiggled about at the car door trying my hardest to remember the few tips Foye had shown me. Thankfully Mercedes these were not and after a few niggles at the lock, the door lock popped up and the car door opened. With that we both jumped in, and I went to work on the casing mechanism. Within seconds I got the engine started. As soon as I heard the engine roar, I jumped out, quickly swapping seats with Gibby and we were off heading out of the street.

Gibby's driving was very erratic. Suddenly it dawned on me, I wasn't the only one telling pork pies that night. He could not drive for shit but by then it was too late.

We came out of Lethamhill Road and as we headed down towards Cumbernauld Road I fiddled around with the tape deck trying to play a tape of happy hardcore music, I had brought it with me just to set the mood.

I remember having this strange sense of achievement at the time. Pleased with myself that I had not only managed to get into a locked car, but also successfully accomplished stealing the fucking thing. Unfortunately for me though all these good feelings of excitement and joy were soon turned to horror and fear. The moment we turned out of the street we had just taken the car from we saw, clear as a bell, a fast-approaching Police car racing down the road towards us. It drove down past

Barlinnie prison and onto the street we were just coming out of at the time. Lights and sirens wailing.

Fuck, I thought, just as that Gibby took off at speed. Not that it made any difference, they were virtually right on top of us. Gibby put his foot down and picked up speed, but the polis by then were almost bumper to bumper with us. A big no-no in Scotland. The police are under strict orders that if a situation is endangering anyone even the defendant, they are to back off.

Unfortunately, we were out of luck. This idiot thought he was a Formula One driver and had, in that moment, forgotten all his basic training.

What happened next would have turned their blood cold, at least I hope it did.

We raced down the short road from the street we had just left and headed straight for Cumbernauld Road with the polis car hot on our heels.

Gibby at the wheel, eyes fixed firmly on the road ahead and happy hard core blaring. My stomach was in my mouth the whole time. I knew we were in the soup here. There was no way we could outrun them. Then Gibby had this bright idea to take a very sharp corner that would in theory take us back onto a residential street with the hope that they would back off somewhat. The move would also have us heading back up to familiar surroundings. Unfortunately, his attempt and calculations were, to put it lightly, in vain.

The corner was far too sharp to take at the speed. He must have been doing sixty to say the least. The move slammed us into the side of the Vogue Bingo Hall. Crash, bang, wallop, is about all I remember. From there everything went black. For how long honestly, I don't know. This was followed by the deafening sound of the engine over revving and at roughly the same moment my vision started to come back to me.

When I came round virtually the whole windscreen was splattered with unmistakable smear of blood. For a spit second, I thought Gibby had been killed. I had visions of him lying slumped over the wheel totally lifeless. I knew I had to look over at him, check out what the score was, but every bone in my body was telling me to just close my eyes tight and not look.

All this would have happened over a few seconds I'm sure but to me it felt like hours. It's not the first time this had happened to me when you're in a position like that time stands still.

Finally, I got my courage up enough to look over only to see Gibby had nothing more than a bump on the head. All that blood had come from me. My nose has always been like the Hoover Dam, ready to gush at a moment's notice. One small tap and the bloodshed is ridiculous.

With us both hitting the wall at that speed there was no doubt we would have been sent flying forward towards the windscreen. Gibby's fat belly may have just been his salvation. There was every chance his belly acted like a self-made air bag sending him crashing back into the driver's seat. God Almighty, using your belly as an airbag! Not even MacGyver could have thought that one up. Whereas I was like a skeleton with a skin graft and was thrown forward at speed, hitting the windscreen and knocking myself out cold and of course, fracturing my English rose "nose" and leaving a bloody mess all over myself and the car.

Even if I had walked away from the car that night without the polis behind us, it would have only been a matter of time before they were chapping at my parents' door the car wasn't exactly short on my DNA.

As I sat there looking over at Gibby. He had turned as white as a ghost, probably thinking along the same lines I had and thinking I was the one who had died.

By the time we got our wits together the car doors were ripped open and the two of us were violently dragged out and slammed to the ground with the handcuff's getting slapped on us both. Forget the fact we had almost gone through the wall of the bingo hall.

Thankfully the more senior of the two officers noticed my injuries and said, 'We had better get this one to the hospital,' said the one

For just a burst nose,' said the more junior of the two.

'He's still losing blood,' came his reply.

The junior of the two simply shrugged his shoulders with an I-don't-give-a-fuck expression on his face as they brought us both to our feet. Unfortunately for the bold Gibster, his injuries were minor and he was carted off to Easterhouse police station there and then. As for me, I got the honour of getting to sit inside Glasgow Royal Infirmary on a Friday night for no less then four hours. This was how busy they were.

It was just another Friday Night in the city that's never sober. The three of us, myself and the two police officers, sat there surrounded by drunken men, emotional woman. Even one or two regulars who just loved to take up the NHS's time; a supposed stroke this week, perhaps a heart attack the next - we all know the sort.

The officers decided to pass the time by trying to find out why some wee sixteen year was running around Glasgow stealing and crashing cars? My response was short to say the least,

'No comment,' this brought the conversation to an abrupt end.

Finally, my name was called, 'Have we got a Paul Alum here?'

I was taken into a bedded cubicle were a doctor stood waiting. What a waste of time. He stood there appraising me with his Xray eyes and pronounced,

'He's fine.'

I was left thinking, is that it? You're not even going to feel my nose before making your half assed assessment? All I could do was stand there stunned and in disbelief thinking, You're a goddamn disgrace of a doctor do you know that?. Of course nowadays things are different, these guys, although still considered to be pillars of society are worked beyond what should be humanly possible hours. The two polis I was with were, I'm sure, delighted as it meant no more standing around in the hospital on a Friday night. As the three of us walked through the long corridors heading back towards their van one of them muttered to himself 'All that for a kid with a broken nose. Aye right.' This only fueled my growing hatred towards all thing's authority.

The remainder of that weekend was spent within two police stations; Friday and Saturday in Easterhouse's station before being transferred to Baird Street's station then directly on to Glasgow Sheriff Court on the Monday.

The size of that court blew my mind. There were row upon row of very slim cages that morning. Within which sat countless boys, girls, men, and woman all hoping to be released on bail. For me and Gibby this was not to be. After a five-minute appearance before the beak the two of us were remanded into custody for the next five weeks.

It was just before 10pm when we finally hit Barlinnie, exhausted and just a little bit pongy. We were booked in and placed in one of Barlinnie's many dogboxes also known as a holding cell. For me this was just another day at the office. I had been through the reception area a few times by then and was starting to become a bit seasoned. Then there was Gibby who might have had a small problem. The fact his old man was a Screw in A hall of the same jail could have been a little red flag. It tuns out no one gave a dam. Not in Barlinnie, Polmont or Glen Ochil. You see Gibby's dad wasn't your run of the mill screw he was an okay guy and every knew this.

After a few weeks young Gibby was released on High Court bail then after the five weeks I spent on remand we were both returned to court where I was sentenced to four months and Gibby, I believe, got three months. This would not be the last time we were to stand on the dock together with the next time being the High Court and none of us going home that day.

THE PARTY IS OVER

The morning the law finally came calling was an anti-climax, no bells and whistles, nothing like that. I never even saw them coming.

One guy did stand out. I don't know why but there was just something off about him; the way he was trying not to look at me gave me that gut feeling.

Honestly, my thinking was more enemy, giving me the vibe that he posed a threat rather than polis. After all, I had only been in court the morning before, so I thought there was nothing to worry about on that front.

But still I had this right bad feeling. There was something about the way the street looked so was empty, it was eerie.

It was a Friday morning around 8am, and back in those days it was possible to get your carry out of booze and ciggys at this time. It was also giro day so you would usually see all the old boozers who stood there daily, real hardcore booze heads that would be getting the shakes by this stage. You could bet your boots there would be a small crowd of them all standing outside the shop, getting a few cans in them before heading out for the weekly giro. On that day not a single sausage was standing there.

Now the chances are that this was pure coincidence and had fuck all to do with them lying in wait for me, but these are the things you notice, small things that were out of place and stood out.

So, there I was. I'd just turned seventeen a few months prior and unbeknownst to me about to start my new life as a Scottish prisoner. The only thing on my mind that morning was doing my usual waking up, eating breakfast and getting drunk. My drinking by now was becoming out of hand. I was also taking a lot of blues and high strength diazepam, so my decision making was dull at best.

This had become my life; ecto's at night to go up, blues to come back down and all of it washed down with booze. By then I wasn't having much fun. I had managed to fuck so much up that I was almost welcoming it. I had broken up with not only Kelly, a girl I was serious about, but also my whole crew of mates.

Jay and I were at each other's throats over everything. It got to the stage that even spending the day together was torture whereas months earlier we were like brothers - and we only had ourselves to blame.

That Friday night, me and Stacey Lennox stayed at my mother's house. We planned to come into Cumbernauld for me to make my court appearance at Airdrie Sheriff Court then shoot back into Glasgow after.

I had been hiding out through in Glasgow for a few weeks after stabbing Davie Young, the so-called Glasgow hardman who couldn't take a joke. Given the weeks had ticked by without any polis coming to the door, I felt it safe to return home and even make an appearance in the dock.

My attendance at the Airdrie Sheriff Court was on some small time beef – nothing to worry about but it would have presented a prime opportunity for the police to catch me.

When we left the Court, instead heading back into Glasgow, we decided to go out and see who was kicking about in Seafar.

We bumped into Jay, John Duncan, and a couple of birds, that's females not the feathered variety, and started getting drunk.

I was also selling Valium at this point and had brought 50 through with me the night before. Instead of meeting the guy we had arranged to meet we did our usual and started getting fucked up instead.

After a very uneventful evening we all went our separate ways, oblivious to the fact that this would be the last time we would ever be standing together again.

Fate stepped in and looking back now, we were never to the same again.

I took Stacey back to my mother's home only to find out she had the horn. She was shit out of luck. I was mad with the drink and had my ex, Kelly on my mind. The conversation had turned to her when me and Jay were talking privately - he told me that Kelly wasn't in a good place since we split up. That made me feel bad. I did love her and didn't want to hurt her – Kelly was a decent lassie, the antithesis of Stacey who came with the excitement of running round Glasgow.

My head wasn't in a good place by the end, and I was pushing everything and everyone away from me. So regardless of what she was wanting I was going to sleep.

I awoke the next morning to my mother banging about, waking my kid brother up for school. We both got up. I looked at my phone and noticed four text messages, all from the boy wanting his blues also known as diazepam. I phoned him and told him I would get him at the shop in an hour.

The worst mistake I've ever made, though chances were they would have got me at the house anyway.

As my brother left for School, I put the blues in my pocket and told my mother I was going to the shop only for her to say that she needed fags and that all of us, that is her, Stacey and myself would go. Shit, how was I supposed to meet this guy with my mum standing right there?

Fuck it, I decided to take the chance. So off we went. As I shut the door that morning, I had no idea it would be another four years before I would walk back through it again.

Before I knew it, I was in the cross hairs - the ring of steel getting tighter around me, and I was completely unaware of what was about to happen even though I still couldn't shake that gut feeling, but it wouldn't have done much for me by then anyway – the polis were ready to pounce at any given moment.

Inside the shop I told my mother to hurry up and get her fags so she could get back down the road and to take Stacey with her.

As soon as they were gone, I banked the blues, or to put it another way, pulled my tracksuit bottoms down just to below the bum line and stuck them up my arse. Why I did that is still to this day somewhat of a mystery. Maybe I thought I was about to be robbed? It wasn't because of the polis because I was still very much in the dark on that one. Whatever the reason it couldn't have worked out better for me. I walked out the shop, sparked my can of Miller and started the short walk back home. I would never do things like drink in the house, especially at 8am.

Anyway, I had hardly cleared the stairs outside the shop when here comes this guy again. Only now he's not trying to blend in. Now he's picking up speed and coming right at me.

Fuck this I'm off.

I drop my can, turned to run and suddenly the street was full of polis. I mean, it was a bit surreal to say the least. Maybe it was a slow week, and they were bored? Whatever the reason I was finished for a few years anyway. Fuck. As it turned out, nearly all of us were simultaneously arrested the following morning leaving only John Duncan on the streets. The friendships were well and truly fractured

The actual arrest was over and done within a blink of an eye. Only I still had one trick on my mind or up arse.

They took me back to Cumbernauld police station and officially informed me that I was been charged for the stabbing of Mr Young then lobbed me into a cell.

I had only one request - a glass of water. As soon as they gave me a drink and shut the door, I pulled the balloon from the crack of my arse opened it up and gubbed the lot.

That was the fastest weekend I have ever spent in the police cells and the cherry on top, apparently, I pissed all over the cell to the point they had to move me or physically carry me into another cell.

I was told on the Monday morning before boarding the court bus about what happened to the cell from hell from this big, baldy prick who dished out more than a few slaps over the years. He got left on clean-up duty. His face was bright red with anger as he filled me in on my actions and there was fuck all he could do as I was getting loaded onto the safety of a court bus. That was it, time to take one last view of Cumbernauld, and just like that I was away on the bus along with everyone else. From that day forward I would be a prisoner.

POLMONT (NOV 2001)

It wasn't just me and Gibby heading to prison that day. Handcuffed next to me sat Mark Tortolano and another guy called Wiggy.

Wee Mark was a Cranhill native, their gang was called YFC through and through. Whereas Wiggy came from Parkhead, although he mostly ran around with all the troops in Bellrock Street. Wee Mark was a good guy, no doubt about that and Wiggy, was a fantastic, fun-loving kid with a great sense of humour. He was the sort of boy you'd be happy to do time with. His lust for life would always pick you up especially if you were having a dark day, maybe sad news from home, girl troubles or just be pissed off in general. No matter what, he always gave off a glow that made you feel better about yourself.

Exactly how and why Wiggy started to run around in Cranhill on the first place is still a bit of a mystery. I'm sure he had his own pals in Parkhead. Or perhaps just like me he was a bit of a scheme bouncer, going from one housing scheme to another on the lookout for good times. Whatever the reason, I for one was more than happy he joined us.

Both him and Mark had been picked up the previous Saturday in a stolen car. There were also charged with a few other daft things but what they were who remembers?

I say daft things; they must have been serious enough to warrant the courts the powers to remand them into custody.

Either that or the judge in question was just a dickhead that day! This of course is only my opinion.

On that day in court, me and Gibby were leaving the dock having just been remanded and there, standing outside the door of the small courtroom waiting to go in were Mark and Wiggy. They had had a long day's wait in the cells and then it was their turn to face the bench. They both came away with a five-week remand each.

Small remands of this length where common in Scotland at the time. Most people appeared in front of the courts on summary charges along with previous convictions, especially ones of the same category. So, if they happened to be standing in the dock they would generally, though not always, be detained and sent to prison to await trial.

Mondays, for the best part, were one of the busiest days. There were all your weekend detainees coming from police stations scattered across Glasgow. Added to which, the beginning of the week meant there were always new trials starting so it wasn't surprising that the courts would have been packed with guys and girls, some walking in off the street, along with as those brought in from prisons across the country. Then you had to factor in all the legal staff; the lawyers, barristers, judges, and day to day admin people so most of the building was packed. Suffice to say that all the courts across the land were a complete nightmare on that unholy of days. Monday. Bob Geldof's famous song, 'I don't like Mondays,' had a point and was potentially inspired from doing a stunt in the god forsaken cells. Most courts were like that after the weekend. Glasgow sheriff! God almighty, that place was just insane with rows and rows of people all stacked in together like sardines. It seemed to never end. This was my first impression anyway.

Away back at the beginning of the millennium standing there that morning looking down the long walkway of cells I could just about make out a large box-like cell set apart. At first, I'm thinking, *please God let them put us in there, give us some room to breathe at least.* Then I found out for myself just what this cell was for.

'That's the bar cell wee man,' came the voice of an old con sent down from custody. Me being young and inexperienced turned and said, 'What does that mean?' The cell had a row of bars on the face of it that led me to think this must be where its nickname came from.

Most of my thinking at the time was based appearance, though when I said that out loud everyone there roared with laughter. 'No son! That's where they put you when it goes tits up and you're left waiting on the Barlinnie bus to take you back up the road.'

Unfortunately, I was to become intimately familiar with the inside of what was known as the bar cell. I'm sure it's true name was nothing more than simply just another holding cell. To all the regulars, so to speak, it was commonly known as the hell cell especially if you were unlucky enough to have had your application for bail rejected.

The four of us all ended up getting remanded that day. Well, that night anyway! It was around the six o'clock before we even got to stand on the dock. This was how over stretched they must have been.

Standing on the dock that night I remember seeing Stacey Lennox, she sat there with old Frank, an old school rascal of my mother's and one of her fondest friends. He stayed in Govan at the time not far from the court itself. So, to save my mother all the time and hassle of having to head into the city just to sit in a courtroom all day and then watch me get sent to prison,

Frank decided to help my mother out. I'm assuming Frank thought; I'll do Angie this favour. So, he sat there to hear my fate and called her after I had been up to tell her the outcome.

The chances of me coming home that day were very low at best and everybody knew it. I did feel bad as I stood in the dock, especially for old Frank, I could see the pure exhaustion on his face. Everyone looked drained and half asleep- all caused from being stuck inside a courtroom watching one person after another getting bail or jail. I'm sure it took its toll, not being able to leave on the off chance I was taken up at that very moment. Even then, it would be a quick one-minute hello/goodbye glance at each other before being whisked away.

After hours of being stuck in the cramped overcrowded court cells for what felt like days, we were all put on the Barlinnie bus just before nine at night heading for prison. Thankfully due the fact that the screws all wanted home themselves. There was no messing about in reception area and we rushed through hitting D hall the young offenders wing around ten at night. What a bloody day! All I wanted to do was sleep. I was drained both physically and mentally.

There was nothing left in the tank, and what I was left with I tried my hardest to hold on to so I had just enough energy to make my bed, and strip down to my Barlinnie Y fronts.

Now these pants where something else. Ripped, white, men's Y front underpants that had been worn by 3000 inmates before you and passed on from prisoner to prisoner. You hoped they got washed in between, otherwise you were getting hit with these so-called white men's Brigit Jones specials. White Y fronts with a big dirty brown strip across them, if you get my drift. Thankfully this unhappy turn of events only ever happened from time to time. The choice was to either wear the disgusting undies or just go commando! Hell would freeze over before I was putting another guys tighty-whities on.

Finally, we got booked into D hall. The screws decided to put me and Mark in together not because we asked; there just happened to be an empty peter. We ended up sharing a peter together for the remainder of our remands. Despite running around together on the outside there's something to be said about living in each other's space, or right on top of one another that allows you to truly get to know a person.

This was never truer than in Barlinnie, their cells were so small you had to leave the room just to change your mind. Also add being locked up twenty-two hours a day into the mix and its either a recipe for disaster or a strong friendship.

I found that me and Mark had a lot in common and an even bigger surprise, he didn't have much time for Stacey Lennox. This shocked me, as when we were on the outside, they always seemed very close. He told me many more things about her, some good some bad but none of it will be getting added to this book. Afterall, none of us are perfect!

We spoke sometimes into the wee hours of the morning on many topics. Lots of talk as you could probably guess was based on getting back home. Sometimes we would just sit there for hours fantasizing about the outside life we were missing. We would plan crimes to commit on our return to society, party's we would have.

Another favourite pastime was rating females, who was the best-looking, things like that. Mark probably had the best-looking girlfriend in Glasgow too. She was a real stunning looking lassie called Debbie who came from the Shettleston area. She could have been a model and for some made reason loved the bones of him. "Lucky wee shite" Mark who looked like a walking skeleton. He was that skinny I would tease him calling him Skeletor or the walking Halloween costume. All in good fun of course - yet he pulled a wee bird like that! Life's a trip sometimes.

One day as we sat eating lunch Mark asked if he could come through to Cumbernauld on our release?

'You know Smithy I just want to see for myself what it's like and all that!'

Now this could have been a big problem to say the least. The problem was Jay, he hated him with a passion and wanted his blood. This I knew all too well. The reasons behind this I just cannot go into here. So, to keep the conversation flowing and not dampening the mood I played along, knowing that it would have probably never come to pass.

I was vaguely aware that there was another potential problem; what if Jay ended up in here with us? After all he was causing carnage outside on an almost nightly basis. It was bound to end up with a spell of incarceration. So, there was every chance he could end up getting remanded and put into the same side of the hall we had been living out our wee remand on.

What could I do? If it was anyone else, I would have been right in there fighting alongside him - but standing tall with Jay I would have done without a second thought. Okay me and Jay where still on the outs with one another but no matter what, he was still like a brother to me. Whether or not we were on talking terms at that moment was irrelevant. I would have never stood against Jay. No matter who it was against. Like I've already said, me and Mark had become very close over that past year; dubbed up together running around in the hall together kicking around on daily basis. Still though if it came down to it, Jay was my main man and that was that.

Thankfully for me nothing ever happened. Jay dodged a bullet remaining free and eventually the five-week mark rolled around and we were returned to court. What ever happened to Mark who knows, though he must have gotten out as he never came up to Polmont with me and Gibby. Same for Wiggy he had been on the other side of the hall, so we never saw much of him through the rest of our time on remand.

However, on the day we had all been returned to court they put all four of us in the same cell. That was the first time we had been together since our initial arrest. All of us bar Gibby, he had been released on High Court bail a few weeks previously and was by then up the stairs waiting to get called to sit on the dock alongside me with the hope of getting out. It never worked out that way for him unfortunately and he was returned to prison with me.

Getting sentenced for us was over in second. The moment Gibby sat down beside me in the dock the judge got right down to business. We hardly had time to say a brief hello before we were told to stand up for sentencing.

'Mr Alum,' as I was formerly known, 'You may only be sixteen years old but it's plain to see you're already fast becoming a repeat offender and even though your offences are still small, it looks to me that you have no respect for the law. I feel a custodial sentence of four months in a young offender's institution would be appropriate here.'

Then he turned his attention to Gibby. 'Mr Gibb you're also heading to prison today for three months.' From there we were both taken down to the cells expecting to be returned to Barlinnie to await a transfer to Polmont the following morning.

Well, this is how it would normally go but due to fact that Gibby's father, Big Gibby or Gibby Senior as he was known, was a serving Barlinnie prison officer, young Gibby was moved up to Polmont that very night.

During Gibby's three-week remand he was moved to Greenock prison because of his association with his dad. He was only there for a few days then moved back to Barlinnie because Greenock was overcrowded.

Gibby was transferred the same night the rest of us were put on the Polmont bus. To me it was a better to get settled as soon as possible rather than be shunted from pillar to post. Once settled, all you have ahead of you is your liberation date, or lib date as it's more commonly known. We all sat on this old, modified minibus sometimes used to transfer prisoners between jails. These buses looked normal from the outside but had barred windows within.

We sat silently inside handcuffed to one another accompanied by four or five screws. Suffice to say we weren't going anywhere but directly to jail.

Sat on the seat beside me was a wee guy I would go on to know very well indeed. His name was William Dickson a great wee guy from Ruchill and to whom I would be pals with for years to come. It's funny, it was only a few days after I'd been sentenced and was facing a long stretch when me and Willy got talking about it, he was due for release in a few days and by coincidence happened to say,

'You never know Paul; you might be standing at the end of your sentence one day while I'm just starting my own LTP sentence (long term prisoner sentence). We both laughed. I remember thinking, *watch this space you've just jinxed yourself. This is going to end up happening to you!* And, low and behold four years later, just a few days away from my release date I was sitting in C hall in Shott's prison and who walks in? Wee Willy with a five-year sentence above his head. I was stunned. I could hardly believe my eyes. No sooner had he seen me the first thing to come out his mouth was, 'When are you due out Paul?'

When I told him, we both just stood there pissing ourselves laughing – a small comment made years back had suddenly come to pass. It's funny the hand life deals you.

My first experience going into Polmont was a mix of emotions, excitement, wonder and even a little bit anxiety, although not so much fear.

I think after coming from Barlinnie, one of Scotland's most notorious prisons, other jails didn't even come close. Even the hall we were in, 'Westwing,' looked a lot smaller compared to that of the over-crowded halls of Barlinnie. Though the noise levels were far worse, ghetto blasters, people shouting across cells and landings, the racket within an echoey building all merged into one big sound. Well, with sixty or so young offenders all in the one hall what do you expect?

As I stood there that first day, all I could think was, *this hall is a fucking asylum*. Then what did this say about me? Within five or ten minutes of being there I had already become one of the tribe. Willie showed me around, introducing me to a few boys, mostly from the Ruchill area; all good boys – I got on with them immediately.

After close to an hour of being in the hall a screw walked out of his office which sat in the middle of the building. He announced it was time for the lunchtime lock-up. This gave the screws a chance to do a quick head count before serving a hall of hungry boys their lunch. The mealtime lockups were never usually long, ten to fifteen minutes maximum unless there was a problem with someone.

When the head count was done, the guards would open the cells of a few select boys to work on the hotplate to allow them time to get set up and go on to serve your food. Then the bulk of the other prisoners were all unlocked and lined up against the wall waiting to go down to the dinner hall.

Polmont used to be, as far as I'm aware, an old Borstal with the screws running it to the same routine. Of course at that moment in time I knew nothing about any of this. I was a new face, an unknown nobody just trying to navigate my way through.

Scottish jails are nothing like people make them out to be. There are boys who will talk tough, telling stories of their time inside, and who will make out Scottish prisons are more like the Shawshank Redemption. Total nonsense. The young offenders were bonkers in the best possible way. A bunch of young kids all running mad, full of carry-on. Some would make out the food was terrible, but this was just an over exaggeration as far as I am concerned.

Or maybe I'm just the wrong guy to be asking. You see, I learned my appreciation for food from the kitchen table at home. My mother is the heart and soul of our family, but in the kitchen, she's less 'soul food' and more 'search and rescue mission'. A visit to her culinary disaster zone could leave you thinking the potatoes fought back and the spaghetti sauce was out for blood.

Asking Big Ang for a coffee was like rolling dice with fate; you never knew if you'd get a cuppa or a crime scene. My standing joke was that her cooking could get her a stint in the kitchen crime court, with the judge sentencing her to probation or a hefty fine. Me? I fantasized about swapping her burnt bangers and mash for prison grub – even a 100-year sentence might have fattened me up then.

Despite my pleas, the judge never saw the horror of my mother's kitchen first hand. Instead, I did time—mercifully short compared to the life sentence of enduring those meals. When I got out, I grabbed the chef's hat, turning kitchen nightmares into dream dinners. Still, those early food frights left their mark; I joke about it, but I reckon if the judge had sampled a bite, he'd have exiled me to a life of ready meals from Angie's Hell's Kitchen as a safer bet. Instead, he sent me to prison for six-year sentence with another four years to run concurrently. Thank God Stacey came along upon my release.

Now-adays I've been a chef for years and it's me showing them how to cook. Unfortunately, the trauma of those earlier days never left. The scars just run too deep! These of course are all jokes.

Tales of brutality and routine beatings by the screws at Polmont are rife, though concrete evidence is scarce. It's whispered that these guards relished in their daily torment of young inmates, but not all fit this mould. I cannot claim to have witnessed widespread abuse, yet I would be remiss to say it never occurred or that I was spared entirely. The screws, on the whole, maintained a semblance of fairness.

One notorious figure looms large in my memory: Mr. Fish, or 'Fishy' as he was nicknamed. His penchant for inflicting pain was not limited to physical assaults; he derived a perverse joy from annihilating any semblance of hope we clung to, often obliterating personal items with a particular zeal for ripping apart photographs of inmates' children. My own encounters with his sadism were in the restraint before a march to the punishment block, the infamous 'digger'. As Fishy, with a small group of North wing staff, rained down blows upon me, I realised the dark heart of the place.

Thankfully though that experience was still a few years away. At the time I was still housed within the under eighteens hall with no real sentence time hanging above my head; a few months at best with only another five weeks still to be served. All this stemmed from one stupid move - being caught within a stolen vehicle. The sad news for me meant this was to keep me detained over Christmas. My first but not my last.

My first Christmas inside wasn't what you would call very festive. The build-up to the actual day was by far much worse than that of the day itself.

The wooden xmas tree was replaced with steel doors, the tinsel with metal bars and Santa with screws dressed in white shirts, black ties, black bottoms, black shoes. Instead of a red sack slung over their backs they all carried big key rings full of grey square like door keys looking dishing out foul language or sarcastic remarks. Imagine the shock you'd get if you ever tried sitting on any of their knees. A Santa's grotto West Wing was not.

The hall itself was considered one of the more modern halls despite no toilets fitted inside the cells. It had been fitted with light switches, electricity in the cells, plug sockets and even TVs which could be taken away at a moment's notice as a punishment.

As far as going to the bathroom Polmont prison was still very much in the dark ages. During the daytime if you needed a bathroom break you had to ring your bell. This would light up a yellow lightbulb above your peter's door, then you had to wait about an hour for a screw to come round to your spyhole and hopefully let you out to relieve yourself. God, forbid you had diarrhoea, or you would be in the shit! No puns intended.

At night, the halls were secured, but a timed system allowed solitary bathroom breaks. A beep hurried you along. The somewhat modern electric system would automatically unlock your cell door at scheduled intervals, indicated by a key code box with red and green lights embedded in the steel door frame, tamper-proofed by welding. Beyond your door, a cast iron gate discouraged any unauthorized wandering.

Returning to your cell required a glance through a spyhole, entering a changing code to trigger the light from green to red, signalling it was the next person's turn. Despite the restriction, you had the essentials: power, a TV, and a kettle. However, during the holiday season, the non-stop Christmas programming on all five channels served as a constant reminder of the family and loved ones you're missing out on, often stirring up loneliness, frustration, and even violence among the inmates.

I remember calling my mother first thing Xmas day morning. All she could do was cry down the other end of the phone. This went on for the first ten minutes. It became a pattern she continued year after year.

With Christmas day over the tension within the hall cool downed a lot. There was only thing left to consider, the bells or as it's called in Scotland, Hogmanay! No real worries there if you had enough savvy and just a little bit of balls.

Getting in a parcel of pills maybe even some of that horrible hash along with some blues to come from the sweeties and you were good as gold.

Not to blow my own trumpet here but when it came down to getting stuff into Polmont I was a fucking master. Smuggling drugs through the visit room, over the fence, in the post, inside devices, you name it we done it all.

Of course, this happened over years not days. And certainly not during that first sort sentence I ever did. This was Hogmanay and was different back then. The bells was always a big deal. Something had to be done but what?

Luckily for me and all the boys doing time then that the staff working within the visit-room area were either incompetent, downright stupid, or just plain lazy. Virtually everything and anything was getting smuggled through the visit room daily. Drugs, lockbacks, phones and my personal favourite booze.

The young offenders back in 2001 was the place to be. Still though at this point in my life all I was interested in was getting in the one and only parcel I thought I would ever take in. The thought of sneaking anything in on my person made my stomach flip with anxiety. Prior to that the only thing that even came close was taking lumps of hash from one country to another as a kid I smuggle personal bits through the airports up my ass for a couple of hundred pounds - adding to my spending money. It wasn't quite midnight express just doing someone a favour from cash. This was a big ass room full of screws, visitors, CCTV everywhere a million eyes watching. Could I whole my nerve? Would I even want to?

Then the day came a friend of mine came up with one massive party bag full of drugs, Es, hash, blue and yellows, Valium, even speed, all double wrapped into condoms. The thing was as big as a pool ball. I just looked at him and thought to myself, *you couldn't flush that down the fucking toilet how the hell can I swallow or even bank it?* Thank goodness for underpaid uninterested visit staff who clearly didn't give two shits what was coming through. All I did was stuck it in my pocket and kept on enjoying the rest of my visit. Finally, last five minutes was called and as guys kissed their girlfriend's goodbye and everyone wished their family's a happy new year, my heart started thumping in my ears, sweat ran down my back. This was it!

Then I thought to myself, *I'm already in prison what more can they do if my mate gets out the door okay? So, getting caught isn't going to have much effect on me one way or the other.*

As we all lined up at the bottom of the visit room doors waiting to be taken back to the halls something happened that surprised me. Twenty odd boys were just walked through and right back to the hall. No search, no nothing. Just lined up outside and marched back with one big ass smile on our faces. I wasn't the only part time smuggler in that room that day. To this day that was still one of the best new year's I'd had locked up. The full hall was dropping Es an hour or so before lock-up. By the time 10pm came round the whole place was rocking, listening to our small radios and talking shite out the windows to one another, even having a wee sing song. We rocked it into the wee small hours with even the screws doing their nighttime rounds laughing and shouting up to the windows of Spay hall, 'They ecto's must be good lads!'

A couple of weeks following that night I was due for release - this would be the only time I would walk out the gates of that fine establishment. Well perhaps I jumped the gun on walking out the gate!

On the Friday morning of January 7th, 2002, I awoke a free man. My small stay in Polmont had come to an end all I had to do now was get walked down to reception, change into my civilian clothing and be walked off the grounds. Only the hall staff were taking their sweet ass time to come and collect me. Why is this? I asked time and time again. I figured that reception must be busy; they will get you when they get you. Finally, after almost an hour my name was shouted and off, we headed down to start my liberation.

The second the reception door swung open there sat in plain sight was a white A4 piece of paper stamped with the heading Strathclyde Police Arrest Warrant with my name on it. I was devastated. On top of all that I had to spend three full days and nights in the cells before going to court. What was it for?

Facing a £100 unpaid fine, I was told by the understanding officers that I'd likely spend a few days in jail before a Monday release. Despite my protests, I was handcuffed and escorted to the police car. However, as we arrived at the court, my worry proved unnecessary. As the garage shutter halted, a court officer approached and ordered my cuffs removed. My mother, unbeknownst to me, had paid the fine. One officer quipped about being a taxi service, and we shared a laugh as I walked free to find my mother, Aunt Sandra, and Uncle Vinnie waiting.

It felt good to be home although freedom felt fleeting; so much had changed during my absence. Tragically, Stacey Lennox's mother had passed away, this was one time I felt truly sorry for her, but it also meant that I'd lost a key alibi in my up-and-coming trial. Carol had given a detailed statement as to my whereabouts in relation to the McCutcheon case. Despite not attending the funeral, possibly still incarcerated or due to its private nature, I was soon back in Glasgow, reconnecting with friends, including Gibby. Although we had shared the ordeal of sentencing, something had shifted in our dynamic. Gibby had been placed in a different hall to me as he was over eighteen, but I could tell almost instantly that he didn't want to be around me. I don't think it was because he disliked me, though that could have been part of it, I think he knew that it was only a matter of time before I was back in trouble. The High Court trial was a few months aways - we should have been keeping our heads down but instead, we were running about like a bunch of cowboys robbing everything that wasn't nailed down. Gibby was still around, still coming up but something was just different. Within weeks, my actions would lead me off the streets.

RELATIONSHIP WITH MY FATHER

To give you the background on my father I feel it important to bring this into the book. Father and son relationships are important and have a bearing on how young lads grow and become men. For my part, my father left before I was even born – unfortunately he chose the bottle over his family and friends despite all the people who were there and would have been there to help him.

Consequently, I grew up with a very low opinion of my dad and saw very little of him. What I did see was a drunk on the street who couldn't stand on his own two feet. To me he was an embarrassment and a fall-down drunk and I felt let down.

At the time I didn't have the words to articulate how I felt and so it manifested itself in the form of aggression. My feelings towards my dad were alien to me an unknown territory that both scared and angered me.

My mother didn't want me to have anything to do with him and worked hard to make sure that we didn't have significant contact. She and even railed at me if I so much as mentioned him. Just saying it would with bring her hackles up, she would see it as being disloyal to her; this would leave me torn between the two of them.

Our relationship changed when I first went to jail at the age of 16. My father started to write to me on a weekly basis, more so sometimes. Initially I wanted nothing to do with him or his letters, but curiosity got the better of me and I began read them. At first, they were light and 'how are you son' type of letters but then, given I wasn't responding, he must have realised that I needed answers and so he began to open. After about 6 to 8 months his words began to sink in. I was beginning to see that what he wrote was truly heartfelt and genuine. Credit where credit was due, he never missed a visit – no matter what institution I was incarcerated in. Polmont for example, was a fair trek to get to, especially if you didn't have your own transport. Polmont was nothing compared to getting up to Shotts, now that was the real nightmare and yet time after time he appeared, never late, often sober and the relationship grew from there. He showed his commitment and through that his love.

Prior to this form of communication I had not had the opportunity to express or examine how I felt. I was shut down emotionally and found it hard to open up and express myself.

Communication is such a powerful key that should never be underestimated. I believe this is at the heart of problems for young men today especially. This need to be macho and make out nothing phases or affects you – this is where the danger lies, leading to all kinds of trouble and ultimately mental ill health and potentially suicide.

With the relationship with my dad, I've always regretted that we weren't closer, that we didn't open up with each other when he was still alive. It's weird how the moment he was gone I was left with a million things I wish I'd told him, a million questions I wish I had asked him, but hindsight can be a cruel thing particularly when it comes to relationships that run deep and aground.

Admittedly I carried a lot of guilt around our relationship which presented itself in my behaviour. It wasn't until many later years when I became mature enough to fully comprehend the gravity of its influence, in particular addiction and its impact on a family and especially myself.

However, one of my happiest memories happened in the weirdest of places – in a prison visiting room and involved alcohol. Polmont back then was far from strict when it came to searching visitors. I used to get small 30p Irn Bru bottles and get folk to bring them in to me filled with whiskey and topped up with just enough Irn Bru to cover it.

On this one visit, my dad turned up, knowing about the Irn Bru scam. I remember it so vividly because it was a blazing hot summer day in July and there he was, this tall, beanpole of a man, wearing a thick Eskimo jacket loaded down to the gunnels - four bottles in each pocket. Honestly, he couldn't have advertised any better that he was carrying contraband even if he wore a flashing neon sign around his neck saying, 'catch me if you can, I'm a walking brewery.'

So, in he came, heads to the canteen and orders his sweeties which are put on a tray and placed on the table between us. Little by little throughout the visit he put two bottles down at a time. Naturally, him being, he couldn't resist trying the juice himself.

So, over the course of the visit and with bottle after bottle getting consumed as quickly as possible, a distinct smell of whisky filled the visiting room. By which time we were both oblivious of the knowing looks from other visitors or just too drunk to care. Our banter got louder and louder as the drink and laughter flowed. By the end of the session, we both staggered out of our respective exits. How we got away of that God only knows but it is without a doubt one of my fondest memories of my dad and something I still laugh about to this day.

LONG TERM STRETCH

I was released in January 2002 after a four month stay in Polmont only to picked up in the February, three weeks later for the stabbing of David Young. This would be the last offence I was to commit. I would not be getting released within a matter of weeks this time, I would be detained for a matter of years.

By Monday evening, I was settled in Barlinnie's D Hall for a week-long hold - Scotland's way of buying time for courts to prep for trial. If indicted, you're looking at 110 days inside before facing the judge.

Stepping into D Hall, I locked eyes with him - the man who'd stabbed me. He was parading around like John Gotti as if he owned the place, a High Court informant with an ego to match. With friends aplenty in D Hall and no plans to keep his secret, I quickly spread the word.

One by one, my mates approached, asking, "What brought you in, Paul?" Each chat ended with the same sign-off: "That guy's a snitch. Someone from Cumbernauld's serving ten because of him." The news spread like wildfire, and soon he had dubbed his cell door for his own protection. I had to laugh, even when hiding he was standing at his window shouting the odds, making threats that I was getting it, and he was the one to do it. I guess he took me stabbing his dad to heart!

Within probably 3 weeks the whole hall started filling up with Cumbernauld boys, John McMillan, Jay was in and John McMillan's co accused returned.

As the days progressed and getting closer to trial certain truths came to the surface. One day while I was playing snooker John returned from his lawyer's visit. His face was like thunder, eyes slit and focused on his co-accused. I watched almost in slow motion as he picked up a snooker cue and slammed the fat end right off the side of his co-accused's head. Then John simply dropped the snooker cue and walked away just like it was another day at the office. Jay and I were shocked. Just hours earlier they were best of friends. What brought about such a quick turn around?

John's answer stunned me.

'Paul, he's a fuckin rat. That bastard has turned Queen's Evidence against me.'

I could hardly comprehend it. The lad had been standing in the hall like nothing had happened, fully aware of what he had done. Rats never get away with their deeds, this is an unspoken code. The fact that he thought he could just sit with the rest of us like it was no big thing and no one was going to do anything about it was lunacy.

His day came one afternoon when he was playing snooker in the hall without a care in the world. Someone leaned over the banister on the second floor and poured a hot concoction of boiling water and sugar over the top of him as he leaned over the snooker table to take his shot.

Most of the hot water hit him and he let out a blood curdling scream that echoed throughout the hall. Everyone stopped. This brought the attention of all the screws and any prisoner who happened to be out on the landing at the time. Of course, it didn't take a genius to know that the boiling water had come from above.

The clipe was carted off to hospital and when eventually he came back the boys in the hall collectively gave him their own version of bad treatment – weird, flavoured toothpaste for a start; boys would floss the crack of their arse with his toothbrush. Unfortunately, for the clipe, when he went to court, he got only one year less of a sentence than John. Was it worth it? I doubt it. He will be carrying that mark on his back for the rest of his days.

As for the full committal it passed mostly without much incident although one day will always stick in my mind was when a screw opened my door and said, 'Alum, visit.'

I wasn't expecting a visit that day and was surprised.

'Are you sure it's me for a visit?' Sometimes they would think you had a visit and leave you a full hour waiting in a room before realising their mistake. Then you were taken back to your cell.

I asked the screw, 'Who was turning up to see me?'

The screw called down to the visit room and the response was, 'A girl called Nikki Holland,'

This wasn't unsurprising, Nikki stayed right outside Barlinnie and would sometimes just appear up to the visit. This was back in the days when the visitors would phone up the jail and ask for a visit. Nowadays its different, the prisoner himself has make the visit request.

Knowing I had a visit from Nikki made me happy. She always cheered you up, as I said before, she was one of my closest friends. There was nothing romantic between us, just two close friends having a laugh, only this visit gave me a bit of a surprise to say the least. As I walked into the visit room who was sitting at the table but Kelly. I knew Jay wasn't going for a visit and my first thought was, 'Who is she in to see?' Then I realised she was sitting at my table.

Back in those days all you had to say was a name and they would let you in. Not very secure for the prisoner, not that the prison gave a fuck. As I sat down with a look of complete shock on my face the only question I could ask was, 'How did you get in here?'

She smiled and said, 'I used Nikki's name.'

'Why?'

Inside I was glowing with excitement that she was sitting there in front of me, but stupid immaturity made me put on a false front, a face of bravado. I wanted to say there and then, 'I'm sorry for letting you down. Can we get back together and move on from this.' But I also knew that my own indiscretions would have played on my mind for years to come thinking is she out there doing this that and the next thing.

She took great pleasure smiling and telling me how she was going out with this great guy and how he was such a good guy. She was rubbing it in but then again, he couldn't have been that much of a great guy because within minutes of our conversation we were all over each other like a bad rash. It felt like nothing had happened. I had missed her and wanted her back, but it wasn't going to play like that. We had a sweet moment during that visit, but it didn't go any further.

The rest of the remand passed by – and then we had our day in court.

MY WRONGFUL CONVICTION (2002)

The day was a Friday, the date October 4th, 2002, and unlike most other Fridays, I found myself sitting in Glasgow High Court. The cells had an old American style look to them with rows and rows of silver, grimy bars. It's funny, all the daft wee details that stick in your mind from important days like these. This Friday was like no other. This was the day I would find out my fate. No matter the outcome, I would be sent back to custody. Having only been sentenced to six years a week before, there would be no illusions on my part; walking free was off the table. This I knew. No, the butterflies in my stomach were due to the fact I was one hundred percent innocent on this one.

The rest of the day, if I am completely honest, was pretty much a complete blank. Well, apart from that awful verdict and, more importantly, my mother's reaction. Having to sit there, endlessly waiting for your name to be called over the tannoy system is purgatory. Boredom and anxiety niggling at your nerves as you wait to hear from your lawyer who takes his cues from the acting QC.

My QC was a real Grim Reaper-looking motherfucker, he had this air of smug arrogance that let everyone know he was in control. He only visited you in the cells with type of news you would normally expect to receive in a cancer ward. Not today, though. No, today was different for some reason; he was smiling, looking happy and optimistic. Who knows, maybe his wife was good to him the night before. The lucky git. Whatever the reason, it was very misleading. I took the spring in his step as good news. Perhaps he got a little bit of inside information that he can't share?

The charge in question was a shop robbery. That morning of the court case was long and cold, not just for me, I'm sure, but also for my legal team, family members, a few friends, and even my son Paul's mother who turned up. Fuck knows why she was there? Probably hoping they would send me to Guantanamo Bay. Anyway, whatever the reason, she was there; she turned up every day with the excitement of setting her eyes on me.

Everyone was left sitting, waiting for eleven o'clock in the morning to hit. Unlike myself, they could at least go out for things like tea, coffee, cigarettes, etc. Not me, though. No, I was left in a cold and almost damp-looking cell with nothing more than my half-ounce of Golden Virginia, sitting on the hard wood bench, looking at some graffiti on the wall that read, "Freedom is a state of mind." I never truly understood what these words meant at the time, but then again, I had never spent years in a box before either. No matter what the reason, these words have stuck with me ever since and something I have thought on again and again; being free doesn't only mean having your liberty.

So here I was, left sitting there since the crack of dawn, having been taken down from Polmont YOIs that morning, first light 'to beat the traffic,' I was told. Chained on either side by two old screws.

At six thirty sharp, we arrived on Mart Street, the name of the street the High Court is on. To just sit and wait and wait and bloody wait. The two old yins I was handcuffed to were both nice old guys. Clearly not from the Glasgow area, as both dropped me off into the custody of the court officers to go sightseeing. Two Aberdonian tourists walking the mean streets of the Big City that made me roll with laughter. That was as funny as it got that day.

Thinking back, I could have probably tried my luck at doing a runner, but doing a runner from these two would have just been bad karma; granted they couldn't catch the clap in a whorehouse, but it just wasn't in me to do it to them. Thinking back, I wish I had the balls within myself to run, but then again, all that would have done is put my sentence on hold for the few months I was at large. Plus, the fact that the two old yins might have lost their jobs just wouldn't have sat right with me. As a working man myself, I don't want anyone out of a job, regardless of the uniform they had on their backs. The best thing about it, my wrists back then were that skinny; slipping out of the cuffs was something you would do sitting on the back of the bus going to and from court every day, so coming out of that van, taking to my heels, and heading for the border would have been no stretch at all.

Back in the High Court dungeons, I found myself laughing at the insane possibility that the jury would return a guilty verdict. A guilty verdict on this? This trial was so ridiculous; it would, in itself, be a criminal offense to find me anything else other than completely innocent. There could be only one true verdict here, that of not guilty. Or at the very worst, I would settle for not proven, though even that would piss me off. A not proven verdict basically means they know the person did it, but just can't prove it.

The lies and performance given by the witness, a Middle Eastern shopkeeper were very convincing. The fact that it was all made up for insurance purposes made no difference to her morals or the prosecution case one bit. You see, the shopkeeper added a few extra zeros to the amount of money stolen in the robbery that day, a dirty trick, to say the least, but one done repeatedly by everyone, I guess. The real figure taken that day was closer to £90 pounds than £900. The police, I'm sure, had a real good giggle at that when hearing this one. Every single one of them knew for a fact that this shyster was at it big time. To them, of course, this was good news. For one, it would give the courts much more power in sentencing if they felt like it. They could fling the whole book at me instead of just a few pages. And two, the chances of her getting £300 back from the insurance companies were slim at best but for her to get the full nine hundred doubloons, that lying bitch must have been living in dreamland.

And how, I hear you ask, do I know the true amount stolen that day? Simple, I knew the guys involved, one of them for sure. Best thing about it, if you think the polis had a hard-on for me, well, they fucking hated him, the real perpetrator of the robbery that is - with pure rage and resentment, but who cares, right? One fuck is just as good as another in their eyes.

All that would change though as just a few months later this guy reversed over one of their colleagues' heads in a stolen car. One Detective Lafferty, causing him severe brain damage and loss of taste - I'm sure I read that one in the papers around the time it happened. Who knows, though, maybe his wife is a terrible cook? Maybe he welcomed the fact that from now on, he can sit down to sugar and shit and kid himself it's a three-star Michelin Sunday Roast, or maybe he spends his days spitting on photos of Mr. Foye, blood boiling at the fact he only got ten years. I would love for him to read this, Mr. Lafferty, that is, by the way, not My Foye. Not that I'm sitting here trying to make fun of it. I'm merely making a point. If the polis had done their jobs right to start with instead of making the pieces fit, we would have fewer people like poor Luke Mitchell serving a life sentence for a murder he never committed while the real danger to the public walks among us.

And before you fling this book off the wall, shouting, "This grass is naming names," I would only ever write his name or any name, for that matter, if I knew for a fact that it had already well and truly passed its time of limitations. Not to mention the small fact that he is also now a convicted rapist. I was, and to this day, will always be innocent of that crime. And when I say innocent of robbing that shop, I mean I wasn't even in Cumbernauld at the time. Coupled with the fact I was on the CCTV system in the streets of the Cranhill housing area of Glasgow some twenty-five miles away should have cleared this whole mess up right there and then. Unfortunately, when the police stop playing by the rules, we're all fucked. How, I hear you ask, do I know they weren't playing fair? Well, the small issue of the missing videotape clearing me of the robbery was conveniently lost; that's the one from the street camera, not the shop, though that was another tape that grew legs, so they lost not one but two tapes, small details that were swept under the rug at trial.

Thankfully, this move usually only happens because they think you're nothing more than a menace to society and generally happens when you've pissed them off so much that they'll bring out their full arsenal. Not that I agree with this crap. I mean, come on, they're supposed to act better than the rest of us.

Going back to the day of the verdict and the little mistake made on the court's behalf. If they had, for just one moment, unglued their fat arses from the chairs straining to hold them and done their job proficiently, they would have noticed one small thing. The real perpetrator of the shop robbery was in fact someone they hated more than most. This would have given him an extra four years on top of the ten-year sentence he was already serving – leaving him ineligible for transfer to an open prison. Had he been rightly convicted instead of me then the rape of a young schoolgirl would have never come to pass. This is due to the fact that he would have been nowhere near his date to be transferred to an open prison. To the best of my knowledge, he spends his days locked away with some of the country's worst sex offenders. Best place for the sick fuck.

Going back to that awful day of my verdict, finally, my name rang over the speaker: 'Paul Alum,' as I was more commonly known back then. 'To Court number five.'

Here we go, I thought, *a quick in and out; you're an innocent man here.* Even though I was already serving six years in Polmont Young Offenders for the crimes I had committed, in this instance, I was definitely guilt-free. At least no more time would be added to my sentence, or so I thought.

I stood in the dock with two court officers either side of me, and waiting for the jury to come back felt interminable.

This big screw leaned in close and whispered in my ear, "I've been sat here from start to finish of this joke of a performance, 100% not guilty." This is what I wanted to hear. Suddenly, in comes the fifteen members of the jury, a bunch of stone-faced, judgmental-looking S.O.B's. Right then and there, I knew I was getting sent to prison for years. I was sixteen; my voice had barely even broken yet. And if this was to go the way I thought, I would be a fully grown man before I would finally see my beloved Cumbernauld again.

'Have the members of the jury reached a verdict?' asked the judge.

'Yes, your lordship.'

'And what is your verdict?'

'Guilty your Lordship'

From the public seating area came a scream, and I do mean a scream. I had no need to even turn; I just knew it was my mother. Wee Angie was overemotional, to say the least; by now, she was standing on her feet, shouting at the jury, 'You have all made a mistake.' It was that moment in life when all you wanted to do was let the ground open and swallow you whole. She may have been daft as a brush but has one of the best hearts you could ever wish for. Still, even to this day, she's just as mad but has that massive heart, something I had, unfortunately, chipped and broken in my younger years.

As I turned to be taken back down into the cells, I could barely look my mother in the eye, the pain she was feeling made a hard day just that little bit harder. That was it the day was over. I was to be remanded for three weeks for reports for sentencing.

My mother couldn't even make the sentencing; it was too emotionally hard on her to see her son be given an extra 6 years to run consecutively, as we had been told by the lawyers to expect. My Uncle Vinny and Auntie Sandra made it instead.

On the day of the sentencing, I was still in shock from the initial verdict but knew I had to stand there and receive the sentence given despite the injustice of it. This may have also resonated with the judge passing sentence as he sentenced me to four years to run concurrently. This meant that it did not affect my initial sentence other than on paper and in my opinion the judge saw this trial as the farce it was but could not interfere with the jury's decision. He had the power to sentence me to an extra six years if he so felt. I figure something inside him compelled him to give me a chance and sentence me to a concurrent sentence. Of course, this is only my opinion. No matter what, I left the dock that day somewhat happy somewhat sad; happy that my sentence was not getting increased and sad that it was an injustice to start with.

HIGH COURT

The day was September 15th and there sat in the prison van cuffed to each other was me and Jay it must have been 7.30 in the morning and even though it was the end of summer the mornings were still bitter cold.

The van bumped along the cobbled streets until it reached its destination – Glasgow High Court. We were taken down the side entrance through very big heavy locked doors fortressed by steel gates and security cameras were everywhere. Police stood on every corner as we were led down the narrow staircase and taken to the charge desk where we were booked in and put into American style cell. Passing by them you saw face after face with dropped head and fear in their eyes. You must remember in these courts they can send you away for 1000 years if they see fit.

In the cells we got friendly with a couple of boys from Maryhill. A black boy called Andy and his co accused who had been caught with a thousand ectos. We used to sit every day in that cell for 2 1/2 weeks before we got taken up to the dock. This was due to the fact that there were 4 murder trials running up the stairs and all these guys would come down every day. Truth be told I was shocked and intimidated, here were guys all in for murder giving it the big talk not giving a fuck. These days I know otherwise; it was all talk and bravado.

Jay used to moan like hell about sitting in the cells all day – whereas he could be back in Barlinnie watching tv. Im not saying it didn't bother me sitting in the cell but what did tell me was that all my family were sitting up there day after day waiting on me to appear in the dock only to be sent home again.

Then finally, it felt like it was coming out of nowhere, all the QC's started to appear wearing their court dress. A bunch of small, tall, fat, small legal personnel all wearing long black robes and their tie wigs. This circus began to make me feel nervous, I didn't understand all the protocol involved with the legalese and the legal people themselves spoke down to us with a sense of smug self-importance.

It was a ruse to intimidate and make us feel uncomfortable and inept. Eventually the lawyers came down with a great deal, only not so much for me. The proposal was that if everyone turned against me it would ensure they got a lighter sentence whereas I would be getting sent to the hangman's noose.

I later found out that Jay was going to take the 15 years with me rather than turn Queens Evidence but there were two others who will not be named here, that were prepared to take that step.

After a heated discussion we all agreed that we would 'Sign the Section,' a legal term in Scotland to say that we would all take equal blame rather than one person taking the bullet.

The upshot being we were all sentenced along the same lines with the judge specifically saying to me.

'Mr Alum, I would have been giving you a much stiffer sentence today but given that you are scheduled to reappear in this court again on Monday my hands are tied, and I can only give you a sentence of 6 years today.'

As for the rest of them, Gibby, who had been out on bail, and this was only his second offence, received 4 years. I couldn't believe it. The judge was on a roll. Ginger received 2 years for a minor part and Jay received 7 years though not for his major crimes but because he was acting the idiot in the dock pulling faces trying to impress Nikki. This pissed the judge off to no end and if there's one person you don't want to annoy it's the High Court judge. The smile was wiped off his face when the judge slapped him with a seven-year sentence – which was later taken down to five years on appeal.

After that I turned to see my uncle comforting my mother, she wasn't the only woman in tears that day. All the boys on the dock also had mothers, girlfriends what have you, all of which were emotional. I've got to be honest, getting sentenced was no big deal but seeing my mother in that state cut me deep and I was always truly sorry about that.

With that we were taken down the stairs into the cells to await the prison bus to get back to Barlinnie.

Entering Barlinnie as a prisoner you would all line up at a wooden reception desk where they would ask you what happened at court and from there move on to the dog boxes. Only, today was different for me anyway. Gibby got put into the protection boxes, no surprise there, this was because he was going on protection only that his dad wanted a word with him in private. Then I said my name and he told me I was going in there. To which I kicked off, 'I'm no beast protection case, I'm going in with the rest of the boys.'

There is one thing you shouldn't do in Barlinnie is kick off as they love to pounce on you and bring you down hard. Thankfully for me this didn't although three of them did frog march me right into the box. I was raging. 'Why am I in here. What the fuck is going on. I want answers and I want them now.'

Finally Big Gibby senior dressed in his full prison uniform kicked a pouch of tobacco under the prison door to which point I kicked it back thinking I don't want any favours from a screw.

His reply was simple. 'That's from Gibby Junior, not me and watch who you are calling a screw wee man.'

This kind of shut me up and I asked him 'Why am I in here instead of with the rest of them?'

'Because I've heard a rumour that you are going to slash my son and you're going to do it in Polmont.'

'Look, I don't know where you are getting your information from, but nothing could be further from the truth. You son was a rat, but I understand that he ended up deeper than he should have been and that's all on me, so you have nothing to worry about from me.'

He said something that surprised me. He opened the door and put his hand out and said, 'Do you give me your word?' I must be honest I was glad I was hidden away in the protection cells as I would have been too shy and embarrassed to shake a screw's hand in front of the boys in Barlinnie.

Nowadays they only people's opinion that matters to me is my partner and my kids. It wouldn't bother me in the slightest is to shake a screws hand.

He did take my word but not enough to fully trust me as he happened to mention that he had friends through where I was going. He told me that we were all getting transferred to Polmont there and then largely because he couldn't be in the same prison as his son.

THE BEGINNING OF LONG INCARCERATIONS

Polmont was run through fear and intimidation. The screws were all bullies they also encouraged division – divide and conquer, between the different areas of Scotland. This proved easier to control inmates. My first day there I learned just how much bullies they were for myself.

I was talking to my mate Jay in the other dog box, laughing joking, giving it 'we don't give a fuck' attitude, but deep down we did, when a screw came along and opened my door and started shouting in my face.

'If you don't shut the fuck up ya wee prick, I'll kick your cunt in.' As I stood up to get to grips with what he was talking about he took this as me challenging him as a square-go. I was half waiting for the punchline thinking *'Is this a joke?' Or is this guy being serious?'* No sooner than that they guy slammed the door and marched away. This left me thinking was Gibby's dad making phone calls turning the screws against me? Is this what I'm in for?

I know now that this was not true, and I think that this guy was just a prick in general and thankfully I never ever saw him again.

From there we were stripped, put in prison uniform, and marched up North Wing also known as Argyle Hall and banged into a peter together me and Jay with nothing to stare at but blank walls. Everything bare, a piss pot in the corner, no electricity, no nothing. *Fuck me*, I thought, *is this real time. Is this going to go on for years? Nothing could be done about it now. It is what it is.*

Eventually we got opened up for rec and the chance to use the phones. I remember thinking *fuck, I'm going to be on the phone to my Ma, listening to her greeting and bawling.* Only when the phone was answered on the other side there was my mother pissed as a fart with Kelly in the background and who else was sitting there but Stacey Lennox.

I couldn't believe it. I was in shock, how much shock can the one guy take in the one day? I've got my brother on the phone trying to speak to me, Kelly trying to grab the phone off him, then Stacey trying to grab the phone off her and in the background my Ma's blazing talking garbage. What a scene!

Disgusted with it all I put the phone down. It wasn't until the next morning everything hit me. Lying on the top bunk of my peter looking at the cell door, an old grey door with studs in it and bars on the windows. The windows had Perspex plastic and the bars were grid style and four blank walls. Suddenly it all hit me, this was life for the foreseeable future anyway.

In the canteen there was a big square, old fashioned telly affixed to the wall. That morning I sat along with my other cell mates watching as missiles hit Iraq in the first invasion after 9/11. It was surreal. It's funny the memories that stick in your head, but I could tell you everything about what was going on in the canteen that day.

Polmont was always bad for slashings. There always someone getting slashed for one thing or another. One time will always stick in my mind, we were in the showers, me Jay and another boy from Greenock, there was also a fourth boy. As soon as I walked into the showers, I saw the razor in the boy's hand but I knew we had no beef so I had nothing to worry about. We had been in the showers on a few different occasions and had a laugh but this time, the boy had a razor in his hand, and that was for no reason that I knew, I was alerted to the fact that something was about to go down.

I gave him a wee nod in passing and he gave me a cheeky grin back. I stepped into the only free cubical which just happened to be right between the boy and the boy he was intending to slash. Within seconds he lunged past the wooden barrier in the cubical right past me at the other boy. For a moment I thought it was for me and my wee arse went tight. Thankfully he went right past me, but godamn he did not miss the boy. He caught him right from his neck, across his cheek right up to the nose. Still the worst slashing I've ever seen in a Scottish prison. The blood poured over the walls, it hit me and even hit Jay on the side as he ran out bollock naked right into the middle of North Wing in front of maybe seventy boys shouting, 'I've been slashed, I've been slashed.'

I felt sorry for the poor bastard because everybody in the hall started laughing, I don't believe it was on account of the slashing, more because he was running about the hall with a bare bum. The female staff didn't know where to look although I would be shocked if they didn't take a wee sneaky peek.

With that he was carted off to hospital, I can't remember if they gave the poor bastard a towel. I hope so. I only ever saw the guy once after that. Jesus Christ the scar on his face was horrendous – but that was Polmont for you, a complete and utter powder keg that was ready to go off at any moment. Frustrated young teens full of carry on, bravado and sometimes violence.

But Polmont wasn't always just violence and carry-on, for the most part it was just boring day to day, more of the same. Once I found my feet, it took me a couple of days to start getting in trouble and then it was four or five times a day, mostly for stupid shit. Admittedly there were some real headcases in there, Nori Carlton for example, was completely bonkers in matters of violence against YO's, screws, anybody, he didn't care. It's safe to say he was the top boy in the jail at that time anyway.

Jails in Scotland aren't like what you see on tv – there is no structure, no king at the top. Nothing like that. Mostly what you see day to day is boys chasing drugs. In this sense I was a master at getting drugs in. I thought up some cracking ways and they always worked.

One time that always makes me laugh was when my cousin's boyfriend at the time came up and flung over the fence a 2-litre bottle filled with vodka, a bag containing 40 ecstacy pills, a mobile phone and a charger. At the time we were in a hall called 'Nevis Hall'. Basically, the prison's thinking was to put all the bad eggs in one basket. What a disaster that was! The hall got wrecked daily, but one thing that was fantastic about this hall was that it directly faced the fence and all we had to do is get somebody in the gardeners to stand in a certain place at an exact time to collect and pass it in through the window.

On this day in particular, the morning parcel came over at 8.45am. I sat there nervous, sipping my coffee waiting on it is coming over then bang right on schedule over it comes. Jackpot! Wee Si Stewart from Maryhill grabbed it and stuck it right in his bin and walked into the hall and passed it in through the window. In return I gave him 5 ectos.

All the boys that were getting some of them knew it was coming that day and sat eagerly waiting and with that a shout came from my cell: 'The eagle has landed.'

I had already swallowed three ectos and gulped back some vodka. As soon as we were opened up all the boys piled into my peter. We all drank vodka and swallowed ectos. I phoned the blond one to brag, laughing down my illegal phone, to say I was drunk and drugged at that time in the morning.

Suddenly a call came out from one of the screws – shouting out all our names, all the party people. We had totally overlooked the fact that we had an education session that morning and were marched off. We sat in the art class barely capable of focusing on the paper in front of us let alone take in what the tutor was saying. Not long after that the tutor figured out, we were all out of it and shouted out to the screws, 'They're all on drugs in here.'

A screw entered the room, his gaze swept across us and then he started pissing himself laughing. What more could he do? 'Look at the state of yous, it's not even 10 in the morning and you can't even see straight!'. Needless to say, that was the end of our art session and we were all taken back to the hall and locked in our cells. Not long after we had our cells searched. I knew this was coming. I had 2 ectos left but hell, could I handle 2 more ectos. I was damned if I was going to let them get it or allow it to go to waste. So, fuck it, down the hatch it. I think I spent the rest of the day talking to the curtains.

This was an everyday occurrence – it was largely about making the days pass by quickly and avoiding boredom.

On a serious note, I was sitting for few days afterwards on punishment because they knew we had had drugs and I'd been caught with an illegal mobile phone, so the punishment was to put us into a bare cell with nothing but the walls. A boy from Ruchill called Barry Weston, the funniest boy I think I've ever met, banged on the door, and says I've got a book here Paul if you're interested. The book was called Sammy the Bull and was about the man who brought down John Gotti.

At this point I couldn't read or write a word and I didn't want to admit that I couldn't read, I felt shamed by it. So, I accepted his book, and it sat in the corner of the cell for about a day and a half and then I thought what could be worse than just sitting staring at four bare walls when I could be sitting and taking a crack at reading this book.

Opening that book opened a whole new world to me. I couldn't put it down. The story engrossed me, I could see the story in my minds eye. Granted there were words I didn't understand but still I continued. This, I'm glad to say, has stuck with me to this day and now I've lost count of the number of books I have read.

HMP SHOTTS

How I discovered I was getting moved to Shotts was a bit of a surprise to say the least. For one, you must be twenty-one and two they would usually give you a couple of days' notice. Neither of these were apparent in my case. I only found out from the boy who worked in reception.

What we did find out was that the screws had found out that myself and a boy from Dalkeith, Tony, were planning to stab a screw. This was on account of him calling my Ma a fat whore to her face when she was up for a visit. This was totally out of order – treat us any way you want but treat my mother, a visitor that way was wholly uncalled for.

Security found out what we were planning and decided to get us out of the prison tout suite.

Tony was moved first. Apparently, he was dragged to the seg unit by officers dressed in full riot gear, otherwise known as the musty-mob, and kept there for a day or two. You could hear him shouting from the exercise pens, 'Tell P to be careful' and that was how I got the warning. Within a day or two I was on a prison bus being transferred out and not even given the reason why. I too was given the riot gear treatment. Only they couldn't charge at me because I just put my hands up and said, 'No need for that boys.'

I was aware this was going to happen as the boy on reception had given me the wire the night before, although he didn't mean to having seen my name on the transfer board. He shouted up to me, 'All the best Paul.'

I couldn't understand why he was saying this and asked for an explanation. I was surprised when he told me. At lockup that night I asked the screws and was told 'I fuckin hope so ya wee prick!' and the door was slammed shut on me. The screw in question was Gordon Smith, the biggest bastard in Polmont.

Toni was transferred to Saughton, and I was initially transferred to Barlinnie and then on to Shotts. This was the last I was to see of Polmont – after three years in the place I was sickened with it.

I had an illegal phone and charger and emptied out half my sugar bag to conceal these things. I stuck the bag down with Pritt stick. It worked a treat because I was transferred from one prison to another and so security wasn't as heavy as it would be for someone coming in off the street. I made it through Barlinnie security without incident, but it was to be a different story when it came to Shotts.

At Shotts they put the scanner wand, the sort you'd find with bouncers at clubs, over the sugar bag and the alarm went off. The mobile and charger were confiscated straight away – usually you would be put on report for something like this, but the screws just put it in a bag and warned me not to try that again.

When I first arrived and walked the walkway to the tubes that took you through to the halls the tune from Prisoner Cell Block H, 'walk the line,' played in my head. As I stepped further into the maze of the prison gates were locked behind me leaving me with the sense that I was going deeper and deeper into this dungeon.

The halls in question were that bad, you had two sections, three levels up. So, six sections all in with around twenty cells in each section. The cells doors faced each other so you saw the same face each morning as you came out.

In Shotts, I was bunked next to Big Dougie, a man who chillingly lectured his deceased wife for days for not eating her dinner. Despite such unsettling company, the prison was unexpectedly subdued; convicts, some in for double lifetimes, preferred peace over hostility. It made no sense to make enemies in there.

The rarity of violence did little to ease the tension—it remained a fortress of fear, guarded by imposing double fences, hence its reputation for being Scotland's highest security prison.

Inside, the strict security stifled drug flow, compelling inmates to brew crude hooch—horrible stuff that gave you a hangover while you were still drunk. A weird experience to say the least.

On this one occasion myself, Tony and another guy called Barry were getting stuck into our hootch. We had been brewing it for a couple of months in readiness for Christmas. At one stage we were so drunk we called my friend Nikki. Three drunk guys singing Christmas songs down the phone.

Then suddenly Tony had one of his not so bright ideas and given I was drunk I went along with it. Daft given I was due out in a matter of months.

Carried away with the idea of smashing up our cells we got stuck in and I decided fuck it, I'm going to put my telly through the office window. With my two pals giggling behind me I went down to the bottom of the section and launched it with all my might. To my surprise there was a screw sitting doing his paperwork on the other side. The fright he must have got.

Laughing we ran back to our cells with more mischief in mind and then set about smashing them up. Before long the alarm went off. Obviously, they thought this was the start of a riot. Officers in full riot gear turned up to find our door barricaded. They were not content to let things simmer down, wanting their pound of flesh they were all banging on the other side of the door shouting, 'Have you got any demands?'

'Aye,' we said, 'We want a chicken curry.'

The head screw, Paul Alan, was asking us to take it seriously but we continued our mischief by singing, 'You keep on knocking but you can't come in.' We knew we were in for a kicking for our pranks so just made the most of it.

As we heard the screws taking the hinges out of the doors, Tony and I faced each other and shook hands – knowing full well that this was probably the last time we would see each other again. It was like Custers last stand.

Then the door imploded and a squad of officers in full riot gear charged in, batons raised with violent intent. We took a good kicking that day and I still have back problems to show for it.

We got dragged down to the seg unit, stripped naked and that's the pivotal moment when I thought, 'There has to be more to life than this.'

I lay there freezing cold, without a blanket looking up at a prison window, Just rows and rows of prison bars with bits of Perspex caught in between and decided there and then in my moment of clarity that I was going to change – that this wasn't going to be my life's purpose. Even though it didn't happen overnight the decision and the impetus had been set in motion.

HMP KILMARNOCK

After being sentenced, I was returned to Barlinnie for a few days though I knew I would be transferred at any moment. Barlinnie is nothing more than a big supermarket, you sit on the shelf waiting to be taken away to your final destination. They only question for me was where will I land? Could I be sent back to Shotts, possibly, but would they have me? Probably not. This is the problem causing trouble in prisons, they don't particularly want you back after getting rid of you – either through getting put to another jail or getting released which was the case with me.

Then all my questions were answered early one Monday morning. The door flew open, and a big screw stood there, 'Pack your stuff. You're getting moved.'

'Where to?' I asked.

'Kilmarnock, I think, but I'm not sure, just hurry up.'

Barlinnie screws were notorious for being impatient and this big bastard hated me, I don't know why.

So, hey-up and away we went down to the old dog boxes. This would be the last time of ever seeing them. I never knew it at the time this would be my last time in Barlinnie. Maybe there is a God after all.

We were bungled onto a reliance bus and driven down to a small town called Mauchline in which sat the big jail bowhouse otherwise known as Kilmarnock prison. Looking at this small town as we drove through you just knew all the screws came from it. I was bang on the money although there was a big surprise that I found out later – not only the screws came from this place but also most of the cons too.

I was transferred to House Block 1, LTP's only and in there put into B wing. So far so good, a nice and quiet hall but opened up just a wee bit too much for my liking. Some people might have looked at being a godsend, you go from your peter to the hall to the exercise yard back to your peter and that's it, all you can do to pass the time. Its soul destroying.

On good days there would be boys out with a deck of cards playing games such as Bella, Hearts, Poker etc., and you could get involved with the games easily but most boys played Bella and for the life of me I never picked it up no matter how hard I tried.

Another pastime the boys took up with but I'm very delighted to report that I never once tried, was smack. I'd witnessed too many boys over the years fling their lives away over junk. It's a sad thing to see lives wasting away like that, something I could never see myself doing. Since most of the screws in that jail had previous jobs like pushing trolleys for Tesco, getting drugs into the jail was no big deal. Unfortunately, this led to the halls being overrun with heroin. There was more junk in that jail yearly than there was on the streets. It was terrible. Of course, it wasn't all just junk—there were plenty of other drugs and some ingenious ways of getting them in.

One of the best methods I ever used involved an old Xbox. I'd take it out of the sleeve, remove the disc drive, and here's the real genius part—sellotape carbon paper, the stuff you'd get on the back of the bookie slips, all down to the bottom of the disc drive. Then, I'd put in my parcel, mobile phone, and, if needed, a knife, and sellotape more carbon paper on top, making it into a pouch. Why carbon paper? X-ray machines can't pass through lead, the main ingredient in carbon paper, so when they scanned it, they couldn't see through it. You couldn't be greedy. You had to make the parcel big enough so the disc drive would fit back into its original brackets without rattling about, otherwise, the game was up. Then, before putting the screws back in, you'd add clear glue so they couldn't unscrew it in security. The prison's policy was all about money—if they smashed the box and found nothing, they'd be liable for the full cost of it. This led security to be told by the top brass to avoid doing that at all costs. It didn't take long for cons to figure this one out, and what a time we had.

There was only one problem: you were only allowed one console at a time. So, what could we do? Ahh, there's an idea. Simply go out on the landing and show how much of a klutz you are, one little trip with a dash of choreography, let it come flying out of your hands, and make sure it smashes off every little step on the way down. Then you have to look sad and tell the screws, "My computer's broken—I just tripped on the floor. Why don't you get some wet floor signs there?" The trick was to have a mix of anger and sadness, all the while trying to hold down that cheeky grin, knowing full well you've just taken the absolute piss out of them. I must admit, I dropped so many computers, they shouldn't call me Candy Ball; they should have called me Butter Ball.

We ran this scam for months without a hiccup, but nothing can last forever. People were getting too greedy – the scrap gang must have been making a fortune fixing all the computers and the screws started catching on. Then one day some complete dick head thought he would put in an ounce of smack and a full-sized kitchen knife. What was this arsehole thinking? He just stuck it in there, rattling about. They could hear it. Still, as much as it was a good laugh doing things like that. I personally didn't like Kilmarnoch, I didn't like how it was run, I didn't like these so-called hard locals who thought they ran the jail. These are the same clowns who would hide in their peters in Barlinnie scared to come out for dinner. Not that I've got anything personal against people from Ayrshire – I hardly know anyone from there and then there was that situation with me and that we screw where we were getting hot and heavy with each other – that's a female by the way. We'll get to that later.

For me Kilmarnock was starting to get too much. I wanted out of there; I wanted out there and then. I was sick and tired of B Hall and even some of the people in it. Most of all I was sick of being opened up all day every day, 7 days a week. It was just not a good existence.

Over a few months me and a couple of lads had been brewing hooch. Finally, it smelt sweet enough to taste. Not the best taste in the world but gave you some kick and so that night we all started getting drunker and drunker. For whatever reason this screw had been annoying me for days came over to tell me, 'Get in your cell. You smell like you've been drinking. Have you been drinking hooch?'

'That was all the excuse I needed. I turned and flung a punch connecting with the top of his eye. Then like raging bull out stormed Brian breaking his nose with one punch while I attacked him from the side. All the other screws ran in in response but remember this is not SPS (Scottish Prison Service Screws), they are SACRO and dangerously unqualified to deal with such situations. All they did was push the two of us into Brian's peter at which point an argument started between me and him.

In no time flat a full-scale brawl happened. Brian was a monster of a man and trying to fight him off was futile. He got on top of me, and I smashed a coffee jar and started stabbing him with it while he proceeded to strangle me – I was fighting for my life. I don't exactly know how it happened although my full life I've had a problem with biting my tongue when I get angry, and I believe I might have done this at that point. Whatever happened my tongue got split in two leading me to receive fourteen stitches and still they wouldn't open the door. The blood was everywhere, up the walls, over the floor, over the door. This was a serious fight to the death and if these cocksuckers didn't get in in time one of us was going to die. Probably me if I'm honest. Finally we Graham Lennox went down to the screws and yelled 'They're going to kill each other in there if you don't get in and stop it and I'll be going to witness against yous that you done fuck all.'

Sitting here writing this makes me think back of how much of a bunch of spineless, gutless, yellow-belly bastards they were.

Finally, the door was opened and we were in that much of a scuffle they had to pull us apart only for us to start fighting with them. This was the fight of my life, I've never been in one more vicious before or since. Of course, I required hospital treatment because of my tongue, but I was that drunk I fought them all the way to the hospital and even started trying to fight with them and the doctors in the hospital. That was the last thing I remember. For all I know they gave me a jag in the arse or perhaps I just fell asleep drunk, whatever it was I woke up the next day handcuffed to the bed, my face splattered like elephant man. I didn't even have shoes on. The bastards had left my shoes behind in Kilmarnock prison.

A wee reliance turnkey offered me a coffee and laughed saying 'You're not going to hit me with it are you?'

I wasn't sure what he meant with this remark. He then went on to tell me that he had been part of the team tasked with transferring me to the hospital the night before and he had never dealt with a prisoner so difficult. The fact that they never had the decency to put a pair of shoes on me goes to show just how untrained these people are.

It turned out this wee old turnkey was a very nice man, hard not to like. I got to know him quite well through that day in the hospital and a few months later for a medical checkup. My eye lid had started to dip, and I was told it would never ever recover. If that's all I walked away from, I was lucky.

As soon as I was taken back to Kilmarnock, I was sent straight to the segregation unit, where Brian was, which I knew and for some reason Graham. He was sent to segregation for a month – for what, stopping a fucking murder. Come on guys, what's happening here.

Brian was shipped out to Shott's prison while I awaited my transfer to who knows where. I was getting out of Kilmarnock, that was all I was interested in.

As one month turned into two and two into four, I sat there waiting and waiting. When you're in segregation you must go before the governor every month – which is known as a month rule. This gives the governor time to either allow you back to the hall, transfer you to another prison or keep you in segregation. For me it wasn't that simple, most jails wouldn't take me, apart from one. Glenochle. My transfer was all signed and ready to go when a boy from my past came back to haunt me. You see back in Polmont me, and Tony Geilty slapped the shit out of this wee guy from south of the border. Not that because he was English, he just happened to be a wee bastard of a boy and where was he now. Yes, you guessed it Glenochle. He had us charged with assault, bearing in mind almost two years had passed by this point, it meant that I couldn't be transferred there for security reasons – i.e. I gave him another kicking.

'So where does this leave me?' I asked the governor. Graham was sent back on the wing and Brian had been transferred and only I had been left in the seg unit and starting to feel that I was just getting forgotten about. After four months down there, they reluctantly agreed they would be sending me back up to House Block 1 but obviously not into B Wing. I was sent to A Wing and put in a section down the bottom – me and three other boys from Paisley. The rest of the wing was full of folk from Ayrshire and all bitter protestants as that town tends to be. Whereas me and the four boys Fudgy, Robo and a wee guy called Brownie were all die hard Tims and used to blast our IRA music in sequence one after the other every morning. We used to call it the Republican wake-up call. Of course, this had nothing to do with political beliefs, just a way to annoy them.

We all became very friendly, me and Robo especially, a very hard guy not to like. We stuck together like glue. If they were fighting one of us, they were fighting all four of us. Not that any of them ever dared.

I also became friendly with a boy called Whitey, a right good boy from the Gallowgate and as you can imagine, coming from there he was even more of a Tim than Henrik Larsson. So that was it, our wee gang was set and for the most part there was never any trouble.

LIFE INSIDE

Building up to my release the date, March 31st, 2006, was very nerve-racking. Life inside those walls was all I knew for the past four years. My 18th and 21st were spent in custody.

Not to mention the birthdays in between. I had friends on the inside, boys who became like brothers.

Boys like Tony Gielty, a red headed boxer from Edinburgh with a heart of gold and fists of iron. He was probably the most loyalist and funniest guys I've ever known. To this day I would still call a friend even though it's been over fifteen years since I've seen him.

The adult prisons ran differently, none more so than that of HMP Shotts. In a lot of ways, it had its own ecosystem. There was a barber shop and a cook house where you could make sandwiches and small snacks to smuggle back to the halls to sell for things like rolling tobacco, chocolate, shower gels, anything.

You also had tobacco barons and drug dealers whom if the rumours were true had a screw or two in their pockets. On occasion there were boys selling mobile phones or at the very least allow you access to them if, for talking sake, there was a parcel of drugs being arranged or you fancied having a wee sexy night with the wife over the phone.

There were boys who had mastered the art of making some of the best gut rot hooch you ever tried. Not quite Glenfiddich but it would do. There were even a bookies for boys like me who enjoyed a cheeky wee Saturday morning punt.

All of this was highly illegal, but ignored if there was no violence, or bullying tied directly to the gambling, the phones or even the drug taking. For the most part the screws on shift knew these things were happening and turned a blind eye. The way Shotts ran was live and let live. The Screws had a job to do the cons had a life to live for the most part it ran like a well-oiled engine.

As for the bookie side of it, you would occasionally see some of the screws, especially the older boys, ones who enjoyed a wee flutter, nipping in on the fly to place a bet. These old boys, like a lot of guys then and now, lived for the good old Saturday racing but it would leave them in something of a pickle, when stuck working the weekend shift.

Their day started around 6am for them. This didn't leave much room to hit any of their own betting shops on the outside, instead of missing out on a full day's gambling, they'd go into whoever was running the C-Hall bookmakers at the time. All off record obviously, place a few naughty bets usually on a Saturday morning. Unless there was a big meeting like Cheltenham, the Guineas or the National to get in on a bit of the action.

To them this was a win win. the bookie in question an old Londoner, back in my time of imprisonment anyway, would give the same odds or better than William Hill or Ladbrokes, whatever was best in the paper that morning. Then come out first light to tell everyone what betting shop he was going with. This allowed everyone to write their bets on a piece of paper with the tobacco, acting as the currency. Then they'd get it back to him no later than midday. Allowing the DIY bookmaker time to sort out everyone's bets.

As for any screws coming in for a cheeky wee punt, they by far always won, even if they lost the race, their bets weren't as costly as ours, not because they were getting any sort of special treatment for allowing the bookies to run more for the fact that they bought their tobacco on the outside and so dodged paying the inflated prices that came from the tax prisons levy on everything.

Everything sold inside the walls comes with their own tax. It's a damn disgrace if you ask me. Prisoners get paid a hell of a lot less in wages - around £17 a week plus the maximum £15 PPC 'prisoner personal cash.' The best you can hope for is around £33 a week yet you still pay a far bigger inflation tax. Think of the cost-of-living only a hundred times worse.

So, all any screw with a brain in his head and some steel in his balls would do is buy a few ounce pouches of golden Virginia from their loyal shops on the outside and use it for betting. If they won? They would sell all their tobacco winnings back to the prison canteen for cold hard cash, possibility even making yet another profit back on them too. From here the prison canteen would add it to their inventory and sell it back to the prisoners at their weekly canteen time. For the most part everybody wins.

Finally, you had three hots and a cot every day along with a family visit from time to time. I mean what more do you need in life? Jails like Shotts with sentencing ranging from four years to some poor bastards who just weren't getting back out found their own semblance of routine. It was boys like this who, off their own backs, made life inside as similar as possible to that of the outside. Fair enough the lack of woman was a big one, but you just had to learn to adjust and make do in other ways.

Had I become institutionalised? I wouldn't like to think so. Was I scared of taking on all the responsibilities of the outside life - things people take for granted on a day-to-day basis? I think it would be more accurate to say these things terrified me no end, but institutionalised, definitely not!

My nerves were starting to get the better of me more and more. There's an old saying you'd hear in prison from time to time: 'all sentences come to an end it was nothing more than just a waiting game.' And at last, my number had been called-up.

Before all that though a few of the boys, decided to send me out with a bang! This was usually referred to in Shotts as getting black ball. It's a bit of an urban legend where the boys would grab you spatter you with things like brown & tomato sauce then cover you with sugar. One last hoorah before you say your goodbyes to guys you have known for years. Though like I said it was as much of a myth as getting your head put down the toilet on your first day of high School.

BEGINNING OF THE CHANGE

Eventually the year turned into 2009 only one month and nineteen days until I was out – February 19th to be precise. I knew this time it was different. I knew I was never going back to prison. I had a feeling it would be tough but never knew just how tough it would be. When the morning came I was to be released, my uncle Vinney and Aunty Sandra picked me up. In the back of a car was a bottle of vodka and a couple of cans.

'Tuck into that son.'

As inviting as it looked, I didn't want to make the same mistakes over again. I knew prison was over for me, my old life was over. I truly did have a moment of clarity and opened my eyes for the first time in a long time. So, I decided only to have one can on the way up the road and even that I sipped.

John Duncan was standing waiting on me, how he knew I was being released I didn't know, but there he was. Then we headed down to the pub when it opened. We still had a half hour to waste so decided to go to the off sales and stand in the woodland area drinking a bottle of wine, only for a police helicopter to fly overhead.

John joked, 'There's your welcome home party Paul, I guess they knew you were getting out today and all.' We both laughed, but I knew I was done with everything, and the only way to guarantee it was to tell everybody just how finished I was.

When I told John, him and a few others just laughed it off, 'Aye right, who are you kidding?'

I thought to myself, 'I'll have the last laugh here.'

When the pub opened, we sat down for a quiet drink – when he asked, 'Do you mind if my pal Stacey comes down?''

'Stacey who?'

'Stacey Rice. Do you know her.

'Vaguely. But sure, invite her down.'

I didn't know it then, but John was about to hand me the keys to my future. Stacey had been a familiar face from afar, but up close, she was breath-taking. Seeing her, something deep inside me clicked open. She stood out from everyone else—I could tell right away.

We clicked over common ground, though Stacey was guarded at first. When I offered to buy her a drink and she proudly declined, it was a sassy, independent response. 'No, I can buy my own drink.' I couldn't help but tease, 'Go buy your own drink then—and get me a double while you're at it.' That got a smile out of her, and the ice melted instantly. I was drawn to her, but I doubted my odds—my bookie could vouch for that. However, as the night unfolded, our conversations flowed, and connections sparked.

There was no mistaking it; Stacey was special. I even stole a kiss that first night, but that was all, and yet, I was hooked. In the months that followed, things got serious. This wasn't just a fling; it was the real deal, the kind of love that you know comes once in a lifetime. I wasn't about to let her slip away—I was all in.

Soon enough, we were setting up our own tiny flat. We didn't have a pot to piss in—just an air bed that would sag to the floor if one of us got up—but we had each other, and that was everything. We can't help but laugh our arses off when we reflect on our early beginnings – some of my happiest memories.

One of my proudest moments came when I built our first real bed. The slats had me stumped, so I laid the mattress right on the frame. Stacey, full of excitement, plopped down only to fall right through. It's these memories—of us, building a life with laughter and love—that mean the world to me.

My old man Alex had set me up with a steady job on a building site working for Millar Homes. I stayed with them for a couple of years but never bought into the building site life. However, I needed the money if I wanted to stay free and clear of prison. Could this be it? Could I stay free of things like prison, violence, and all the negativities in my life?

One harrowing night, as I visited my father with Stacey, everything spiraled. An altercation turned violent when a drunken fool, having already terrorized my dad, turned his aggression onto us, we took the argument outside, and it ended up with me being badly slashed.

In the heat of the moment, I floored him with a punch, but his rage was out of control—he called for his girlfriend to stab Stacey. "You'll stab nobody," I spat, just before he lunged and slashed me, carving pain from the back of my neck to the corner of my lip. In a daze, I scarcely registered the attack. "What have you done?" I cried, only to receive more slashes across my ear and below my left eye. Somehow, I knew deep down these weren't paper cuts, blood was pouring from me by the bucketload. Adrenaline surged, and I found myself strangling him, possibly channeling Brian from Kilmarnock? Yet still he wasn't finished and pulled a Stanley knife and slashed me a further three times. The bloody scene turned into a grim echo of another life I thought I'd left behind.

Stacey, horrified by all the blood, called the ambulance.

I told the guy to flee, a twisted act to avoid a return to prison. By the time the police arrived, he was gone, and I was left with a tale of falling on a bottle.

The local hospital, Larbert, was unequipped for such injuries and I was moved to Monklands. The next morning, I was seen by one of Scotland's top surgeons. I lay there beneath the stark hospital lights, aware of the deep scars I would carry—marks that could have spelled my end.

Recovery was more than physical. The incident plunged me into a dark place; drinking, drugs, aggression—it was all there, perhaps PTSD, though I had no name for it then. It cost me my job at Millar Homes, as I struggled with attendance and the psychological weight of exposed scars and public scrutiny.

It was at this crossroads, in the shadow of my old life, that I faced a choice: succumb to the familiar or chase a lifelong dream of becoming a chef. And then, life asserted itself—Stacey was pregnant. Jobless and soon to be a father, becoming a chef was no longer an aspiration; it was a necessity.

Lucas arrived nine months later, and Madison a mere ten months after. Our family was complete, and with that, I sealed the chapter on further children and got the snip. The scars I bear are not just etched in skin but carved into the narrative of a life redirected—towards a dream, responsibility, and a legacy beyond the old ways.

So, in our mid 30's both me and Stacey went back to college as mature students, Stacey to do hairdressing and me to do chefing. I studied three years at college to learn my trade. Our day started at 7am – we'd drop the kids into the Cumbernauld college nursery and then head to our individual classes. As soon as college ended, I would take my whites off put my civies on – head out to the Westerwood and work until 10pm. This went on for duration of my study and could sometimes be exhausting but the bite of the kitchen kept calling me back. Once I had a taste of the kitchen I never looked back. It also made me regret every decision I ever made that took me away from my calling. With all the time I wasted in prisons I could have been building my chefing career. This gang life may look glossy from the outside but trust me, it's a life of misery and disappointment – there are NEVER any winners. Unfortunately, it took me years to learn that.

The kitchen suited me perfectly – a bunch of crazy wee so and so's having a laugh and getting the job done. Even learning a trade in between.

My first chefing job was in the Westerwood Hotel, where I trained under the great Joe Queen. Although I didn't know him at the time, he was one of Scotland's culinary geniuses. He even offered me a chance to go with him when he was moving to Edinburgh.

I hadn't totally missed my calling and started a new job in the Grand Central Hotel in Glasgow – still the best team I have ever worked with to this day. Working in that kitchen was like watching the sequel to 'One Flew Over the Cuckoo's nest.' We had a head chef who was pissed every day. Their walk-in fridge was like a walk in bar – for chefs only of course but this is only the tip of the story. Chefing took me in a different direction for which I will always be grateful. It was what I needed to completely cut myself off from my old life and turn it around.

Today, my life is wholly wrapped around my family – there are no other concerns. I no longer drink or take drugs; I live a clean and sober life by choice and I never been happier than I am today than I am with Stacey and the kids.

Even though this book is full of humour - any kid that thinks this life is glamourous and exciting – think again. I was just lucky to get out the other side. Lots didn't and lives for them and their families were ruined because of it. Achieving your dreams is hard work but well worth the effort. Don't let opportunities pass you by, when you get the chance, seize it with both hands.

THE LAST HOORAH

My last hoorah was more of a sweet surprise. Two ecto's were put in my hand from Tony Roberson an Edinburgh boy who I went way back with to my earlier days in Polmont and one to whom I became very good friends.

All the boys took ecto's that night and the plans were we would spend a few hours at our windows, high as holy hell and have a right good old chinwag about the old days in Polmont.

My last night in C-Hall within HMP Shotts passed by a lot quicker than I expected.

That night we dropped our sweeties half hour before lock-up time. The final time I would hear the door go click. Before that though I was to have one last surprise, a visit from a screw in the Seg unit. It was none other than Mark Cowie a bold headed muscle bond mountain of a man. He had come up from the young offenders not long after me to work in the seg unit. It was probably the best place they could have put him as there was a strong possibility, he would have brought the Polmont mindset with him 'don't tell us we tell you.' This I have no doubt upset the delicate balance.

Mark Cowie was a real hard arse but to be fair to him he was a straight down the line no nonsense sort of guy! You always knew where you stood with him.

I always thought that big lump missed his calling in life. If he had been sent to Barlinnie in the beginning instead of the YOs he would have made one of the top brass. He had that way about him. Usually only seen in Barlinnie.

But back in C-Hall that night, there he stood just five minutes or so before lock-up. 'What peter "cell" is Alum in?' We all heard his voice echoing down the hall. The boys laughed, 'watch this Paul he's here to make your last night that of a night in Seg unit. A final fuck you from the old days in Polmont.'

This of course wasn't why he had come up to the see me. He had come up to simply say goodbye and good luck. A classy act on his part if you ask me.

I stepped out of Tony's peter and gave him a nod. True to form this was the case. He had taken the time to walk up from the Seg-unit to our hall just to say take care and don't be stupid don't come back, go live your life.

That meant something to me. He also had a half smile on his face when he looked at mine, which had been taken over completely by the very strong ectos.

He just smirked and said, 'Jesus Christ! Alum. The night before you get out, really? ' With that, he shook my hand and left.

This wasn't only the last night of my six-year stretch it was also the end of the boy formerly known as Paul Alum.

I decided it was time to embrace my true identity: Paul Smith. 'Alum' was a borrowed name from my stepdad, a label that the police latched onto but one I intended to leave behind. No grudges held, but as I sought a fresh start, the weight of 'Alum' wasn't mine to carry. Yet, the switch to Smith was short-lived; the constant explanations proved too tiresome.

When the call for lock-up came there were a lot of handshakes from all the boys in C-hall with some shouting down 'good luck for tomorrow, Candy Ball.' "Paul". It's funny but hearing all the shouting made me think back, triggering a memory, reminding me of the night before the High court sentencing all those years ago.

Trying to sleep that night was a nightmare, a mix of excitement and chemicals running through me kept my eyes almost stapled wide open. Then after an hour of looking up at the ceiling I drifted off into half-asleep only for jingle of keys to make my eyes spring open.

This was it. Home-time! The screws opened the door doing their first morning count and saw I was up and about.

'Right Alum, get your shit together and we will let you out for a quick shower - if you want?'

I was in and out so quickly that I think I forgot to get wet. This was great. I didn't sleep and didn't come down. It was just pure excitement and adrenaline keeping me going.

Around 7:20 am they shouted, 'Let's go pal.'

'Pal? I am getting out.'

Off we went up through the red tubes along towards reception to change into my all-new clothes. As soon as I was dressed there was no messing about, no sitting in the dogboxes, well Shotts never had dogboxes, more like big rooms, but they never even locked the door to the holding box.

'Soon as you're ready Paul, come out.'

I was like Clark Kent changing to Superman in a phone box - even the reception staff giggled. I was escorted, a short walk, to the main doors to collect my lib grant - a few shillings they give you on your way out. I signed my name for the last time, and I was a free man.

SHORT ROAD TO FREEDOM

Approaching the final gate, I spotted Alex and Craig waiting—but where was Mom? Her absence stung, not gonna lie. I'd pictured this day for four years, and her missing it felt like a let down. Later, learning why she hadn't come, I couldn't help but smile. She'd been in a cleaning frenzy, wanting everything perfect at home, and spotted a few last-minute tasks she couldn't ignore. Still, her not being at the gate barely dimmed the thrill of freedom.

Then with just one step over threshold and my world got a whole lot bigger. I was a freeman for the first time in years. It was a thrilling sensation. The feeling you can only get standing on the right side of the prison fence.

Then we sped off in Alex's car heading for Cumbernauld with a pit stop in Hamilton to check in with my Parole officer - One fat arsehole of a woman just looking for a reason to send me straight back to prison.

Driving into my parents' home street, I saw, at the top of the road, my mother. She had been standing there for just under an hour waiting on my return and was shaking to the bone. I wasn't even out the car yet and already and the tears were streaming down her face.

'It's good to see you mum.'

By now, her emotions had gotten the better of her, and I folded her into my arms with a little bit of a lump in my throat. It was a special and very emotional reunion. Inside her home, her four, yes four, Yorkshire Terriers greeted me in a frenzy and pinned me against the wall. Talk about a coming call. It was definitely one way to kill the mood.

Once the dogs calmed, my aunt Sandra and uncle Vinnie checked in to see how I was and where I was mentally.

Vinnie was aware the adjustments post prison demanded and having done time years before understood the challenges ahead. I excused myself for a haircut, craving a few moments alone to process my freedom.

I left to go the barbershop at the back of my boyhood home. I needed a haircut but mostly I needed just ten minutes to myself a moment to take a breath. As I sat there I caught sight of John McMillan outside. We, along with Kris McGowan, had crafted grand schemes in Polmont. And there were ties made in Shotts, like with an Essex man of certain repute. Yet, the enormity of those potential paths shook me. Could we transform jail dreams into reality, or were we fated to return to our cells?

My pondering was interrupted when John, knowing me all too well, produced a bottle of whisky. A symbol of old habits and a test to my resolve. A drink on day one? Tempting, but not in my parents' home—a place deserving of respect.

Luckily, for the first time in a long time everyone's doors where open to me. Everyone was wanting to see me. My old man had even set up a little bit of a shindig with a few of his friends. So, after an hour in my mother's house Vinnie drove me and John. to see my old man. He did me proud with banners, champagne the works. It was 1pm at the time and I was due to be Cranhill by 3pm. Stacey kept in touch during my stint in Shotts, even offering me a room until I found my feet in Cranhill. My days in Cumbernauld were over; it was time for a fresh start, little did I know what lay ahead.

Stacey's friend, Lisa Park, whom I'd never met, was throwing me a welcome home bash—a generous gesture indeed. I found myself at my dad's place, wading through his raucous party, determined to stay clear-headed while dodging the tidal wave of booze. I was committed to pacing myself—not for Stacey's sake, but for Lisa's. She'd extended a kind hand, and the least I could do was show up to her celebration on my own two feet, steady and grateful.

Navigating the delicate balance of not offending John McMillan or my father, who was clearly thrilled to have me back, became a dance. John's invitation to his place was a thinly veiled detour from family obligations. Despite my father's suspicions, I took it, knowing full well I wasn't coming back I wanted drink drugs and some sweet wee chunk of ass to keep me warm that night.

As we walked to John's flat in the unseasonably warm March sun, our conversation was a slurred soundtrack to my anticipation. In the haze of the heat, sleep deprivation, and the buzz of freedom, led me to getting tipsier than I planned.

Finally, taking a taxi into Glasgow, the transformation shocked me—familiar places were now just memories among vacant lots. Armed with only an address and a vague description of the block of flats I got the taxi to drop me at the tower and made my way from there, The streets were filled with people soaking up the sun on their balconies. A few inquiries soon led me to Lisa's place.

it was teatime, and the scheme was full of wee birds in short, short summer clothes, I mean there I was having not seen females looking like this in a long time heading into the shop to buy a carry-out. Let's just say seeing all these fine-looking young ladies, well thank God they never thought that it was a gun in my shorts. I can see the headlines now,

'Shopkeeper left in in state of fear and alarm after a hardened criminal walked in with what was thought to be a full-length shotgun in his shorts. Honest to God, I would have been the only guy in history to be recalled to prison for a fucking hardon.

The night introduced me to a young lady charmed by what she called my "boyish good looks" and "cheeky grin." We found our way upstairs and got lost in a moment's passion, though neither of us under any illusion about what it meant. Stacey Lennox and I were never more than casual, yet even that was entangled with complicated emotions, bottom line was that we were never compatible.

Looking back, I was more intent on reconciling with Kelly, to offer an overdue apology, not rekindle a long-extinguished flame. We'd kept in touch through my stint in Polmont, our conversations hinting at a visit that never materialized, thanks to a so-called friend's meddling.

Fresh out of prison, I was eager to restart my life, yet I was also aware of the messiness that awaited—a blend of past connections and present temptations, all intertwined with a need to make amends.

IN DEEP

My reputation had spread through the East of Glasgow, catching the attention of two figures shrouded in notoriety—I'll just call them Lego and Ghost. To the world, they were elusive drug lords with the trappings of success that could entice any ambitious youth. When they reached out, it was with an offer that was as dangerous as it was lucrative.

Our first encounter unfolded on Starpoint Street amid the carousing at Lisa's party. Outside was parked a red-headed enforcer known as Lego, who commanded instant respect. I could tell he was somebody even at first glance; I just knew he was a guy on the rise.

'Are you Paul, or is it Smithy even?'

'Yes, mate, I am. Very pleased to meet you.'

'You know your names, good wee man. A few boys who know you from here and Cumbernauld say good things. How would you fancy coming to work for us?'

'Doing what?' I asked. He just smiled and said, 'What I'm told you do best.'

We both laughed.

'We're looking for someone like yourself to do some work. There will be a good payday in it for you.'

'Thank you,' I said. I appreciate the offer, but I've literally just come home this morning.'

'Well, if you change your mind, take my number,' he said, and with that, he drove off.

I was left wondering, *Who the hell was that and how did he know who I was?* Josie came out of the house just as Lego left When I told him what happened his response was, 'Paul if your game for it those boys are running everything in CranhIll just now. If they're offering you work, you would be mad to turn it down. The thought crossed my mind: could this be the step up *I had been looking for?* Finally, after a week or so I decided to give Lego a call.

My nerves were all over the place, and everyone I asked seemed amazed that they even knew who I was. I decided that letting a chance like this pass me by would have been a major mishap.

Lego and Ghost's proposal was clear: run a shop and handle those who skipped payments. I was already tasked with distributing goods from allies made behind the walls of HMP Shotts, men whose influence matched their inside clout. Failing them wasn't an option unless I fancied serious repercussions.

As I waited for the shipment, I was aware of the delicate balance required. Entering Lego and Ghost's territory, an interloper daring to cut into their domain, was risky business. In Glasgow's criminal labyrinth, even small missteps could be lethal. Stepping on toes here meant more than just bruised egos—it was a shortcut to a swift and violent downfall.

I needed muscle, someone to cast a shadow of fear in Glasgow's underworld. Jamba was that man—Paul Ferris's former right-hand and a name that sent shivers down many a spine. With his backing and a nod from Lego and Ghost, we set up our own operation. Life was taking shape; I was rising to what I'd always imagined for myself. The cash flowed, the drugs were pure, and the gigs for Lego paid in hard currency and white powder.

But life has a way of throwing curveballs, and my time was up. Greed and my rash nature clashed with Jamba's paranoia and mental struggles, straining our bond. Yet, by some grace, we reconciled before his passing, his legacy undeniable in the pecking order of Glasgow's heavyweights.

When Jamba and I parted ways, the operation crumbled. Contacts went silent, possibly caught by law, leaving unpaid debts and a dead-in-the-water shop. From flush to broke, I grappled with a spiralling coke addiction and a desperation for more—more money, more highs, a freefall into a destructive abyss.

The expectations piled on, demands grew heavier, until one ominous night, Lego's voice cut through, "Smithy, jump down to Mr Ts house.' My role was the heavy, knocking on doors, heart hammering, hoping the debtor on the other side wasn't larger than my lean frame. Meanwhile, the man known only as Mr. T would wait in the car, safe as houses, collecting half the cash for his role as a chauffeur in this perilous venture. Fed up with the imbalance, I confronted Lego, demanding a fairer split or I'd walk. The dispute ruffled Mr. T's feathers, but it was just another day to Lego.

In the haze of my escalating troubles, an unexpected call from Stacey offered respite. Nikki was inviting us over. It had been years since we'd seen each other, and now, with her own family, Nikki had traded street life for motherhood—a change I could hardly grasp back then.

The cab ride to Easterhouse, to Nikki and her partner Alan, stirred nostalgia in me, a fluttering excitement for a reunion that promised a taste of the old days. Alan turned out to be an instant comrade, a kindred spirit who brought the banter and belonging I'd been missing.

After a day of reminiscing, Alan and I landed in Barlanark. The night spiralled into chaos when a drunken prank with toy guns aimed at an old acquaintance, Coco, got wildly out of hand. Our laughter turned to alarm when Coco ended up in a coma days later, and rumours pinned the blame on us.

The severity of the situation didn't hit until an early morning pounding at the door. The full scheme was abuzz with our supposed guilt. As reality sank in alongside the morning sun, so did the weight of the predicament we found ourselves in—smeared with a crime we hadn't committed, yet jokingly mimicked days before.

Stacey's was blowing up with calls. Lisa, the girl whose home faced the scene of Coco's assault—the same Lisa from my first night of freedom—was amidst a roar of rumours and police lights. She warned that our names were being tossed around by the local gossip mill as suspects in the vicious attack.

Josie's fury was a match for my own boiling blood. Innocence didn't matter; the mere shadow of suspicion could hurl me back behind bars due to the stringent conditions of my release. Being linked to criminality was all it would take for a swift recall to prison.

"We need to get ahead of this," I declared, despite Josie's confusion on how to combat a wildfire of speculation. Hiding was not an option. We donned the very clothes from the night before, down to our underwear—a tactical move for a potential forensic examination. The local CCTV had betrayed me once; I wasn't going to let it happen again.

We set out to confront the heart of the rumours directly, aware of the risks. This was no blind march; we were armed and prepared to defend our names and lives. The stakes were life or death, but for now, survival was the name of the game, and we were playing to win. I had been stabbed before and made a vow no one would ever get the drop on me again. Life had different plans for me, and before I knew it, I would be rolling the dice again with my own life. However, that day any cunt wanting to have a go would be rolling the dice with their own existence.

Stacey's phone was ablaze with dreadful tidings. Lisa, a newcomer to my life, lived at the epicentre of the turmoil outside her door where Coco had been attacked. The morning after, the whispers were rampant: Josie and I were the prime suspects, the talk of the scheme. Josie's indignation mirrored my own outrage at the accusation that could effortlessly cage me once more under the stern conditions of my release.

Resolved to confront the situation, we marched through the streets at 10 a.m., armed not with revolvers but samurai swords concealed down our tracksuits, a brash reminder of our mental spiral. Even with the police likely on high alert, we sang defiantly, Why can't we be friends, aggravating Stacey, which made us sing louder and fuelling our own reckless bravado.

Arriving at Coco's, the door opened to the hard stare of his inebriated mother. My initial fury dissolved as empathy crept in—her son lay potentially dying, and here she faced those accused of his near-murder. The reality of what my mother had endured during my own stabbing resurfaced, and clarity began to edge out anger. I told her straight, with Stacey as my witness that we were wrongfully accused and distanced from any grudge with Coco.

As time ticked by, the wait for retribution was excruciating. We didn't know if it'd be the police, Coco's mates, or family that would come knocking. The blue Ford Focus that sped towards us one day turned tail when faced with our readiness to defend ourselves—it was the closest thing to a confrontation we had.

The truth finally unfurled from an unlikely ally, Coco's cousin Lynn Higgins. A casual boast at a party revealed the real culprits—some lads from a different scheme, seeking vengeance unrelated to us. Lynn's integrity shone through as she relayed the information to Coco's family, absolving us. Apologies never came, but at least we were clear from the blame—a cold comfort in the chaos of our lives.

Lynn and another one of her cousins, I forget his name were the only two that had the decency to come and say sorry. As for Coco I heard that he came out of coma kept his mouth shut and everyone just moved on.

By now, I was almost yearning to be recalled. Don't ask me why. Maybe, like in my teens, prison was where I could finally breathe again. My drinking and drug use had spiralled out of control. From dusk till dawn, all I could think about was booze and coke. The coke was easy enough to come by. The guy who used to be my partner in crime, driving us around while we did jobs for Lego and Ghost, always had plenty of "Charlie" on hand. Even that once-strong relationship had crumbled. Now, I was becoming a nuisance, always wanting more coke from him but never coming up with the cash. Money soon tore us apart, and my debt kept growing. Eventually, everything fell apart. Harsh words were exchanged, feelings were hurt, and two guys who were once friends were now at each other's throats. I decided the best course of action was to split up and go our separate ways. Just like breaking up with a bird, the last thing you should do is crowd each other. After a few weeks, the tension started to ease.

Then, one morning, my phone rang. It was someone who shall remain nameless. They told me that while letting the dog out for a walk, they overheard the driver, as I'll call him, telling another guy that I was in for it.

'That fucking prick Paul is getting it. If he thinks Stacey is his salvation, he's got another thing coming.'

Could this be true? Why would he be discussing this out in the open, with his own house nearby? Truth be told, I never liked the person who called me. He was notorious for causing trouble and then sitting back to watch the chaos unfold. He even got me into a fight with a guy once over something trivial. The guy, Gerry McLeish, I almost came to blows with that day ended up committing a heinous crime that very night, murdering a woman and her nephew in the high flats. I couldn't believe it. Just hours before, I had nearly been fighting with him. It was like dodging a bullet.

With the person telling me this, I was instantly on full alert. Not because of what was supposedly said - that's something I can get to the bottom of later. Was any of it even true? Screw it, I can't take the chance. I better get in front of this. With that, I grabbed my lockback and made my way to his house to confront him face to face. Just ask him straight up.

"You got a problem with me?" I asked him point-blank.

His response was simple, sharp, and to the point. "Smithy, if I had an issue with you, I would cut through all the bullshit and just come around and knock on your door. The way I see it, most things can be resolved with a simple chat over a coffee."

A coffee and a talk? I'm thinking violence, and this guy's talking about milk and two.

His demeanour, his tone of voice, even his eyes were soft. No violence here. It took me by surprise and immediately cast doubt on the credibility of the person on the other end of the phone.

"Look, mate, I'm truly sorry. I got some bad info, to say the least," he said in his now strong Glaswegian accent. "Look, mate, I'm no rat. I promise it was said, and I promise to get to the bottom of it. Even dropping names in a situation like this, I just cannot do."

Obviously, my first response was to call this person back and confront them about the bad intel, at best, or the outright troublemaking, at worst. As I stepped out the front door, I saw my best mate at the time, Mr. Joseph Lennox, sitting in the stairwell. "What the hell are you sitting there for?" I asked.

"Look, Paul, I saw the way you stormed out. I could hear you talking on the phone in the kitchen and knew something wasn't right. I was coming around to make sure you're safe and to stop anything before it started."

"Okay, mate, that all sounds good and rosy, but riddle me this. How much help would you have been from out here?"

He chuckled and said, "My ears work fine."

"Eh, what the fuck does that mean?" I asked.

He never did tell me. I guess if I'm ever going for a hearing test, I know just who to call.

As soon as we got back to HQ, I dialled the guy's number and unleashed a tirade. "What the fuck's your problem, mate? I've just made a right tit of myself and for what?" But he stuck to his story, and eventually, I let it slide, chalking it up to him being a troublemaking bastard. Little did I know, within six weeks, I'd be staring death in the face.

BANG BANG, HE SHOT ME DOWN!

Over the next six weeks, the driver started showing up more and more, always bearing gifts - free coke, booze, cigarettes, you name it. Then, on a spooky Halloween night, as the kids trick-or-treated, I got a text from the driver saying he'd just picked up a big lump of cocaine and did I fancy meeting him as he wanted a second opinion on it. I wasn't going to let something like that pass – what the fuck, I was Joe Cocaine! Forget the party I'm heading to meet this boy. The party was packed with familiar faces and absolutely buzzing, but there was no way I was bringing all that coke in with me. These piranhas would devour it in seconds, leaving me high and dry.

So, I concocted a little white lie. I told everyone I needed to pop back to our flat to grab something, with Lindsay reminding me to fetch the Dr Hook CD. "No worries, pal," I said, and off I went, just down the road to a house, a place agreed with the driver, that was eerily close by. Halfway down Bellrock Street and into the house I went.

As soon as he opened the door, I should have seen the warning signs in his expression, telling me to turn and run. Instead, I charged in headfirst, my mind battling between the voices screaming "It's a fucking setup!" and "Free coke, mate, get in there!" Unfortunately, the allure of free cocaine won out, and I stepped inside, only to hear the click of the door locking behind me, plunging the entire hallway into darkness.

Then came the first punch, and let me tell you, the driver might have spent his time lounging on his fat arse while we ran all over the west coast of Scotland doing X, Y, & Z for Lego and Ghost, but he was also a gym freak and an amateur boxer. And that one punch? It was almost as painful as the bullet itself. In that cramped hallway, there were maybe four, perhaps five men, all jostling for their own piece of the action.

One of them was just there for show. You could see it in his eyes. He pulled out a kitchen knife so big, you could've named it Excalibur. And the moment I saw that, my arsehole tightened up tighter than a hangman's noose.

I've been stabbed before, and it wasn't a stroll in the park. That was with some lockback that felt more like a butter knife compared to the bone-cutter this bloke was waving around. Luckily for me, his movements were more like a dance routine, leaving me with nothing more than a scratch across my chest.

Next up? CS gas straight to the face. Let me tell you, that stuff is no joke. It's like having your eyes set on fire, then dunked in a river. And just when I thought it couldn't get any worse, amidst all the chaos and shouting, I heard those words I never wanted to hear:

"Fucking shoot him! Shoot him now before he comes back on us!"

Suddenly, I found myself staring down the barrel of a revolver, mere inches from my head. Time seemed to slow down, and all I could do was accept my fate. Then, something strange happened. All my fear, all my emotions, they vanished. I resigned myself to the fact that I was going to die in Glasgow, probably rolled up in a rug and dumped in a ditch somewhere.

Then, his hand started to tremble, and I realised this guy didn't have the guts to pull the trigger. Not to kill me, anyway. And just when I thought I was safe, he aimed for my stomach and pulled the trigger. Missing my guts by inches and hitting me in the top part of the thigh. The pain hit me like a white-hot poker, searing through my leg. Finally, my survival instincts kicked in, and I fought my way through the attackers, slamming up against what I thought was a locked door.

When I reached for the handle, it swung open, and I stumbled out into the night, my head spinning. My journey to freedom was far from over. Someone mistook my head for a log and brought down a hatchet, splitting it wide open but if that was the sharp end, I was in the morgue not the ICU.

Pure adrenaline kicked in and I took off running to the flat where the party was. Blood was pouring from my head, and I was found it hard to see. All I could think about was reaching the safety of the party. Somehow, I reached the block of flats, fell into the stairwell and hauled myself up the stairs using the railings to pull me up to the second level. I left a trail of blood behind me. I banged the door with my hand and when it was answered I fell in muttering. 'I've been shot.'

Immediately, someone phoned 999, hysteria behind their voice saying, 'My friend's been shot in the head.'

With blood pouring from my head wound, it's easy to see how they mistook it for a headshot. In the chaos of the moment, anyone could've made that mistake.

It felt like seconds before the whole of Cranhill was swarming with armed police. They were everywhere. Inside the flat, the party guests were all herded into one room while the Police searched for firearms. When it was my turn, some bigshot with a terrible attitude pointed his rifle right at me, barking orders. "Lift your hands," searching me for a firearm. Being the smart mouth I am, I decided to give him a piece of my mind. "I'm the one who got shot, ya prick."

"I'll bloody well shoot you again unless you calm down, your cheeky bastard," came the reply.

He was the one aiming the gun at me, so I calmed down. Eventually, they let the paramedics in, and I was carted off on a gurney to the waiting ambulance, surrounded by a crowd of onlookers eager for the drama.

Now, my mother, that's a whole other story. Stacey Lennox rang my mother's house; she was working a night shift at the petrol station at the time. Alex drove to pick her up and tell her that I'd been shot in the head. My mother, in a frenzy, called her boss, who told her to lock the station up and get to me.

In Alex's panic, he must've called my uncle Vinnie and Auntie Sandra who taking the motorway, raced into Glasgow so fast they left my mother and Alex in their dust. Despite all the turmoil between me and Stacey, the real issue I have with her is her telling Alex I was shot in the head. By that time, she knew full well it was just a leg wound. The head injury was nothing more than a scratch.

Finally, they all arrived at the hospital, only to find me sitting up and talking. My mother's face turned as white as a sheet. She thought a bullet to the head could only mean one thing - she'd be identifying my body. Honestly, who could blame her for thinking that. Most folks don't walk away from something like that. As a father myself now I can totally relate to her worries.

Their visit was over in minutes, but the CID wanted to talk to me. However, just as the doctors informed me of their impending arrival, my health took a sudden turn for the worse. Funny how things like that happen, isn't it? Pain and discomfort conveniently cropping up when you need them most. I knew they'd be back. Especially considering this was a shooting, back in 2006 when they were much rarer than they are today. Even now, they're still uncommon.

So, bright and early the next morning, in walked a couple of suits. It's not enough for CID officers to get their wage rise or a pension boost – these pompous pricks showed up decked out in their finest suit and tie – appearance is everything? At least, that's how it was back then. Nowadays, you've got these CID rookies still sporting their first tufts of bum fluff on their chinny chin-chins. Imagine getting convicted based on evidence from someone whose balls haven't even dropped? Not back then, or at least, not these two.

They came in guns blazing, assuming I was somehow guilty. I guess they figured, "He's done time, so he's dirty either way." Thankfully, just as they were laying into me, the doctor arrived. I seized the opportunity to ask the doctor to order them to leave. Even the police must obey a doctor's orders, especially in a hospital. So, grudgingly, they stood up, warning me they'd be back that night, expecting me to spill my guts. Did they think, because of my North Lanarkshire heritage, these tough Glasgow cops would intimidate me? Yeah, right, piss off, you pair of pricks! But I knew they'd be back, and they'd probably have a word in the doctor's ear about me supposedly wasting their time and exploiting the hospital's duty of care.

What to do? Screw it, my mate was coming up for a visit later that day anyway. So, I called him and asked him to bring me something to wear and help me slip out. Jay was more than happy to oblige, and within the hour, I was dressed and out the door. Leaving the police with nothing but an empty bed to interview. They must have been raging.

After about a month or so, they tracked me down. Well they just became a pest, coming back and forth to my mother's home. I was hiding out at my uncle's, so they weren't finding me anytime soon. After taking as much crap from my mother as I could handle, I eventually caved.

'When's the next time they said they would be here?' I asked. Whatever the date was, I don't remember. I sat there and just told them, plain and simple: 'Look, I hate cops. I'm telling you nothing, so just piss off.' They tried to push, of course, then tried to bargain, all the usual crap they do. Then finally, they gave up, made some stupid comment on their way out the door, and I never heard from them again.

I may have been free from them, but the lousy bastards contacted my parole officer to inform them of the shooting and insinuate it was due to my criminal nature. They had no reasoning for this, none I could think of anyway. This was a bad move on their part, aiming to have me recalled back into custody. So, when my parole officer told me she needed to see me right away, could I come up now? I knew that Cumbernauld police were probably standing right beside her. That's how they do it. These dirty tricks have been used for a millennium. Only this young whippersnapper was just a bit too quick, and I took off, mostly hiding in my dad's flat, sometimes in Falkirk, sometimes in Glasgow.

Then Stacey told me something life-changing: she was pregnant. I never did get to see my son being born. I was arrested two weeks later, with drugs and a lockback knife. This meant I was getting recalled and going back to prison – they used the lockback and drugs to claim that I was associated in organised crime and within weeks I was settling into my peter in Barlinnie looking at a two-year stretch.

THE BIRTH OF MY FIRST BORN

The birth of my second son, Paul Jr, happened while I was in Barlinnie prison. Not the most romantic setting to hear you've become a father again, but there was no one else to blame here but me. My reckless actions led to me being recalled back to Bar. My mother had phoned the prison in the morning to ask them to pass the message over to C/hall that I had, for the second time, become a father again. Barlinnie was notorious for not passing messages over to the halls, but thankfully, this wasn't one of those times.

August 04, 2007, was a Saturday, and everything was done first light because it was the weekend. You had breakfast at 8am, two boiled eggs and a buttered roll. Then around 9 am, you could do either exercise or PT. Unfortunately, it was exercising only that day. Off we went, just another Saturday morning walk in an anticlockwise way, something every prisoner in every prison does for reasons nobody knows. It's always annoyed me.

After exercise, we all headed back inside, and as I got to the second landing, there was a screw who just hated me with a passion.

"Alum, come with me," he said.

'What for?' I thought, 'a drug test maybe? Fuck, I hope not.'

One of the boys came in with a lump of hash up his arse, well wrapped, and we had been puffing it a few days now. If it's a drug test, I am definitely failing it; I was stoned at that moment.

"Come into the office," he said. "We've just been given news. You became a father last night to a baby boy. Congratulations, kid!"

I stood there grinning from ear to ear and asked him, "Do you know his name?" Expecting him to say, Vincent.

"Paul Jr," was his reply. I was shocked and very angry. We had already agreed that he would be called Vincent after my uncle, one of my life's most important people. I asked if they would allow me access to the payphones to contact outside. I tried her phone, it rang out. I tried my mother's mobile, but that rang out. Then my mum's home phone rang out.

Finally, around 2 pm, just after lunch, I again asked and was let out to make my call. Finally, after a few hours, people started to answer their phones.

My mother picked up almost right away. "For fuck's sake, Paul, I've been sitting waiting on you phoning all day," she said.

"You have? I've tried you three times. Anyway, forget all that. What's the baby's name? Are the screws just fucking with me? Or has she named him after me? I fucking told her that he was to be named after Vinnie. I'm not happy with that!"

My mother, wanting to just keep the peace, tried to cool me down. "It's only a name, Paul!"

"Well, if it's only a name, then what was wrong with Vinnie?"

Still, by then, there was nothing that could be done. I believe it was a week or so later that they finally brought him up to the visit. I remember thinking, this is just not how it should be. I should have been there at the birth. My mother was, so she wasn't on her own. I may not have been with her, but this is my son, and I shouldn't be back inside. This was yet just another reason why I needed to start making big changes in my life. It was time to grow up.

As we talked and I held the baby, all the screws circled my table like a bunch of sharks waiting to strike. They always kept close attention to guys holding babies, thinking that people were so low-down dirty bastards that they would use a baby as a way to smuggle in drugs. In all the years I spent in prison, I've never seen or heard of anyone using kids of any age to help smuggle in anything, let alone drugs that could kill them. In my opinion, this is just a dirty rumour. Then again, I'm not in every visit, so who knows for sure? Still, though, the screws could do little to lighten my mood. I was on cloud 9, only looking down at his wee face, pure blonde, his big bright eyes looking back at me. Before I knew it, the visit came to an end. I kissed my son, hugged my mother, and shook Stacey's hand.

A few weeks later, I had my first court appearance at Airdrie Sheriff court, only to be given some bad news. Because of my recall from my six-year sentence, I was to be remitted back to the High court for sentencing. This was not good news, even though I was only in for a small charge as crimes go, but it was still the high court. They had much heavier sentencing powers, and here I was, going back to face my fate.

After a few months on remand, my sentencing day came. I was only going up for a knife. Who cares what I was wearing? It turns out the judge did. He even mentioned it while sending me to prison for four years. Four bloody years for carrying a knife. The way he did it was giving me 40 months on top of the 8 months I still had left to serve on my original sentence. I couldn't believe it. I was crushed. Four years for a fucking knife. If nothing else, it slapped the madness right out of me. I was finished. When I came home this time, that's it for me.

ABOUT THE AUTHOR

Paul Smith is now settled with a family. He still resides in Cumbernauld no longer associates with anybody from his former life. He spends most of his time as a chef and working with at risk children advising them of how to avoid the pitfalls of gang and drug life.

If you enjoyed this book, please leave a review on Amazon or Goodreads.

ACKNOWLEDGEMENTS

There are almost too many people here I need to thank, some of whom have sadly passed.

A special thanks to some of the people who have impacted my life in a positive way and whom I wish to mention here.

My mother Angela, stepfather Alex, brother Craig.

My partner Stacey Rice and Children, Paul Jr, Lucas, and Madison.

Also, friends who have by far been with me through thick and thin: Kelly, Jay McCarroll, John Duncan, Nikki Holland, Alan O'May

A special thanks to some of the maddest chefs I've ever met too: At the Grand Central Hotel: Craig, Danny, Gary, the two Davies and Big Naz and none more so than Joe Queen and Paul Clark who showed me what it meant to be a chef. I will always have respect for these men.

And finally, Jose a skinhead Spaniard who would march about the kitchen singing IRA songs, totally bonkers.

There is one special thanks I must give out – if not for this lady this book would not have been written. She has become a friend and much more, she helped with my dyslexia and showed me the wonderful world of writing, I will always be indebted to Lea Taylor, of The Book Whisperers, and wish her all the luck in the world.

Printed in Great Britain
by Amazon